'Social Stories™ provid... ...guidance needed by those who ha... ...facilitate the application of Social Stories™ to the many issues experienced by adults with autism, from employment to managing emotions. The stories will create a ...olidate achievements and facilitate successful navigation of the ... ...nd emotional landscape.'

— Tony Attwood PhD, Clinical Psychologist and author
The Complete Guide to Asperger's Syndrome

'This is an indispensable resource for anyone supporting young people and adults with autism. It applies the well-established strategies of Social Stories™, which have been proven to be highly effective for a broad range of issues through childhood, and applies it to the most pertinent challenges adulthood. This book will guide readers through how to explain abstract and complex concepts related to employment, and maintaining physical and mental health from the perspective of people with ASD. Dr Siobhan Timmins fills a void in the literature by writing this unique book. I cannot recommend it more highly.'

— Marianna Murin, Principal Clinical Psychologist at Great
Ormond Street Hospital, author and ASD & LD Module
Lead for CYP IAPT at Anna Freud Centre and UCL

'Totally absorbed from start to finish and covers many articles that me and my family have experienced or are dealing with. Particularly, the workplace scenarios were very helpful and I could relate many of my son's experiences, and gain support and confidence from. Furthermore, teaching them the importance of maintaining their physical and mental health needs, helps and encourages them to carry on learning and growing. As a parent whose son was diagnosed at the age 20 and is trying to understand the complexities of the autism spectrum, this book will help me enormously to support my son through life challenges that are to come.'

— Debra White, parent

'This intensely practical book offers the missing information young adults seek who are on the Autistic Spectrum when navigating the adult world. The author shows knowledge and insight to the transition to adulthood by sharing how both her professional and parenting expertise have worked both worlds intimately together in helping her son. The content of this book provides an easy-to-follow set of supported guidelines for families and professionals alike to implement the social story concept within their lives and work. This book is also a must-read for any mental health practitioner who take seriously the significant social and interpersonal difficulties faced by those they serve with Autistic Spectrum Condition.'

– Lisa Parker, NHS Neuro-Developmental Mental Health Practitioner and ASD & ID IAPT Therapist

'These articles are exemplars of the important topics which may be introduced pro-actively to prepare for the practicalities of adult life. As life becomes more complex there are often many stories/articles required for each topic. As always there is meticulous attention to the use of meaningful vocabulary and adherence to the defining criteria of Carol Gray's Social Stories™. All those striving to provide the best support and guidance for those on the spectrum will find them inspirational.'

– Eileen Arnold, co-author of Revealing The Hidden Social

'I read 3 social stories from the book. The story about moving from unsettled to settled in the workplace will be very helpful to me because I found that my own experience at work was difficult to cope with and affected my confidence. Reading this social story when I feel unsettled will help me manage my anxiety.'

– Tom, young adult recently diagnosed with autism

Successful Social Articles into Adulthood

by the same author

Successful Social Stories™ for School and College Students with Autism
Growing Up with Social Stories™
Dr Siobhan Timmins
Foreword by Carol Gray
ISBN 978 1 78592 137 7
eISBN 978 1 78450 404 5
Part of the Growing Up with Social Stories™ series

Successful Social Stories™ for Young Children with Autism
Growing Up with Social Stories™
Dr Siobhan Timmins
Foreword by Carol Gray
ISBN 978 1 78592 112 4
eISBN 978 1 78450 376 5
Part of the Growing Up with Social Stories™ series

Developing Resilience in Young People with Autism using Social Stories™
Dr Siobhan Timmins
ISBN 978 1 78592 329 6
eISBN 978 1 78450 643 8

of related interest

My Social Stories Book
Edited by Carol Gray and Abbie Leigh White
Illustrated by Sean McAndrew
ISBN 978 1 85302 950 9
eISBN 978 0 85700 166 5

SUCCESSFUL SOCIAL ARTICLES INTO ADULTHOOD

GROWING UP WITH SOCIAL STORIES™

DR SIOBHAN TIMMINS
FOREWORD BY CAROL GRAY

Jessica Kingsley *Publishers*
London and Philadelphia

First published in 2018
by Jessica Kingsley Publishers
73 Collier Street
London N1 9BE, UK
and
400 Market Street, Suite 400
Philadelphia, PA 19106, USA

www.jkp.com

Copyright © Siobhan Timmins 2018
Foreword copyright © Carol Gray 2018

Library of Congress Cataloging in Publication Data
A CIP catalog record for this book is available from the Library of Congress

British Library Cataloguing in Publication Data
A CIP catalogue record for this book is available from the British Library

ISBN 978 1 78592 138 4
eISBN 978 1 78450 403 8

Printed and bound in Great Britain

MIX
Paper from
responsible sources
FSC® C013056
www.fsc.org

This book is dedicated to my son Mark,
who faces all challenges with
an honesty, courage and dignity
that humbles me daily.

He will always be my inspiration.

Contents

Foreword
Carol Gray

Learning of a child's diagnosis of autism makes time stand still and surrounds a parent with unanswered questions. There is one question, though, that echoes through all the others: 'What impact will autism have on my child's future?' Dr Siobhan Timmins knows this question first-hand. I have faced it, too, as an adoptive parent of two children with special needs. In fact, parents presented with a serious childhood diagnosis know this question and the pervasive fear that it creates. Just as the word 'autism' stops time at first, when the clock begins ticking again it has an unfamiliar urgency. Siobhan has harnessed time well and invested it in one direction. She has used it to create a socially sensitive and sane childhood for her son, and with him has built the foundation for what will be – by all early indications – a happy and fulfilling future.

Successful Social Articles into Adulthood is the fourth book in the *Growing Up with Social Stories*™ series by Dr Siobhan Timmins. In each volume, she has shared the Social Stories and Social Articles that she has written for her son, Mark, from his diagnosis at age two until today. As the person who initiated, defined and developed Social Stories, I am impressed by how Siobhan has internalised the Social Story philosophy and criteria as though Mark's life depended upon it, and how the result of her efforts is giving us much more than a literary collection.

Whenever I am asked to write a foreword, I always do two things. First, I read every word of the book from beginning to end. Next, I review how to write a foreword. In recent years, that means using a Google search to update my understanding. This time, I discovered a to-the-point article, '37 Tips for Writing a Book's Foreword' (Kunz, 2016). The list begins with 'Tip #1: Read the book.' What? Wait a minute! Doesn't *every* author of a foreword do that? Apparently, no. To skip around and read here and there would be like trying to write a book report without reading the book (which, I admit, I *have* done, but not with good results), or patching nail holes in drywall without painting over them. Wall fixed, but… we're not painting?

If it feels like something is missing, it is. It's not the best we can do.

I share this with you due to a concern that I have for this and every volume in the *Growing Up with Autism Series*. I fear that people may regard each volume as merely a collection of Social Stories and Articles, review the table of contents for a Story or two that they need now, and flip past Siobhan's detailed discussion that precedes each. This would be similar to authors who don't know it's essential to read a book before writing its foreword or a painter who only patches. In Social Story terms, 'Sometimes adults may decide to skip the parts of a book that have critical information and long-term benefits. This is a mistake.'

It is all about the details at this stage of the game. Childhood is history and adolescence has passed. Mark is an adult. I found myself holding my breath for him several times. When Mark wanted an apprenticeship, I was frustrated by the requirement of an interview and the other obstacles that he faced, including the competition of several qualified applicants. To the rescue, this volume contains several Social Articles addressing a wide range of frequently requested topics, as well as others that are central to success but often overlooked. Case in point, in a job interview, what is meant by the question, 'Where will you see yourself in five years' time?' Siobhan explains that her son's initial response, '...in a mirror...,' is a reminder to think ahead and share information before it is needed. That's why this book contains sixteen Articles about looking for a job. And several others describing how to keep it, with topics ranging from hygiene to punctuality, to teamwork and offering assistance, and more. Siobhan's insights include the background and rationale for each of the Articles, as well as the unforeseen yet pivotal decisions that she makes to develop each one.

It's a good thing that Siobhan is good at writing Social Stories because she takes them into challenging topical territory. At times while reading, I sat back in curious anticipation. How is this going to work out for her? Take eating healthy meals for example. Often sensory issues are involved, which is enough to humble any Social Story author to use caution. Mark is preparing many of his meals and never grows tired of his favorite foods. I can feel Siobhan running for her computer or paper and pen. Where will she go with this? Siobhan begins with federal assistance, a national guide to healthy eating (I've done that myself!). That fails. She returns and tailors the information to make it meaningful for Mark. I honestly don't think there is a topic outside of the grasp of Siobhan's Social Story pen.

As a physician and parent, Siobhan is keenly aware of the importance of eating right, regular exercise, annual physicals, and emotional health. As a Social Story expert, she is uniquely qualified to share this information with her son and others with autism. I am particularly impressed with her strategy to address her son's anxiety regarding annual check-ups. It's unique in that she uses the current check-up to help her son gather the information they need to alleviate check-up anxiety in the future. Another example of the benefits of thinking ahead while in the grips of an immediate issue. It's a calm genius that is evident throughout the Social Articles related to health, a context where a parent's concern and a child's anxiety may increase.

Sometimes people familiar with Social Stories but not well versed in their use will conclude that while Social Stories are helpful in describing events and concepts, their positive phrasing and objectivity are incompatible with negative topics like divorce or death. To the contrary, as Siobhan illustrates, the Social Story Criteria provide a safe and reliable framework for addressing uncomfortable truths. I applaud Siobhan's Articles about life stories, including 'Mum's Life Story so far' to begin the process of introducing Mark to the end of her own life. The Article contains a description of working through significant loss that I believe will ring true for many people, regardless of their faith or beliefs.

As I mentioned earlier, a review of the Table of Contents reveals a notable collection of Social Articles. Reading the book sequentially from the first words of the preface to those that bring this volume to a close, it's a single inspiring story. In the previous books in the series, Mark is younger. I recognized many of the early issues and appreciated Siobhan's Stories and solutions. Now, I am getting to know more about Mark's personality and character. He's a young man and an adult in his own right.

Reading fascinates me. We can be reading one thing, taking that in, but all the while our mind is busy translating written words into 'what does it mean to me?' That is what holds our attention. After all, if nothing 'speaks to us' we become bored. As I reached the final chapter, I kept thinking that if I was a parent with a child recently diagnosed with autism, this is the book I would want to read first. The discussions demonstrate how a childhood and adolescence of personalized Stories, Articles, and related resources and activities can build a foundation for life. It's a blueprint for parenting a child with meaningful information. At a moment's notice, any one Story or Article – sometimes from many years past – is recalled into active duty to explain a new concept, phrase, or situation, or work alongside a new Article. Siobhan has created a cohesive and accurate record, an encyclopedia that will support Mark for many years to come.

Following the Social Stories philosophy and criteria to the letter, Siobhan is defining something very new. We have Social Stories, yes, but thanks to Siobhan and Mark we have an intervention far more powerful to consider. While I will forever be surprised when someone excitedly shares with me that Social Stories 'work' for their child or client, Siobhan has introduced me to their enhanced power and long-term reach when used systematically over an extended period.

Read this book cover to cover, as I did, as well as the entire *Growing Up with Social Stories* series. It's a practical and reassuring step-by-step answer to what parents can do with the finite time that they are given to work on their child's behalf.

I wish you and those in your care the very best. If this is your first book by Dr Siobhan Timmins, let me congratulate you on your decision to start here. If you've read her other books, well, I knew you'd be back.

References

Kunz, J.C. (2016). 37 Tips for writing a book's foreword. Retrieved online https://kunzonpublishing.com/2016/05/37-tips-for-writing-a-books-foreword-2.

Acknowledgements

I would like to thank Mark for giving his wholehearted support to the writing and publishing of this series of books. Mark wants to make a difference to others in the world and in giving his permission to publish his Stories and Articles I know he will help many children and adults on the autism spectrum and the families who love and support them.

Special thanks must go once again to Carol Gray for developing the fabulous approach of Social Stories™. Her phenomenal insight, enthusiasm and creativity know no bounds. Carol's friendship and continual support throughout this project have been absolutely invaluable. Thanks too to all the team at Jessica Kingsley Publishing for their patience and expert advice, especially Jessica Kingsley herself, whose personal encouragement throughout has given me confidence to continue to write.

Most of all I must thank my husband and family for their unfailing love and support. Thank you.

Introduction

Social Stories™ are known to be an effective evidence-based strategy for children on the autism spectrum (National Autism Center, 2015). In compiling this collection of Social Stories and Articles in the series 'Growing up with Social Stories™', my aim has been to highlight and demonstrate the potential of this invaluable strategy across the lifespan, as I have used it over the last 23 years with my son. The Stories included in the books in the series build understanding of issues of increasing social complexity over the years, from *Successful Social Stories™ for Young Children with Autism* to *Successful Social Stories™ for School and College Students with Autism* and eventually addressing more adult abstract concepts in *Developing Resilience in Young People with Autism* and finally *Successful Social Articles into Adulthood*. These books are intended for those who work with or care for a person with autism.

As an author of Social Stories I have to rethink the responses and behaviour of neurotypical people and revisit them from an alternative autistic perspective, breaking them down into their component parts and finding logical reasons for the things that are said and done. This process is essential for even the earliest Stories explaining the simplest of concrete social tasks, such as brushing teeth, and it continues to be crucial in unravelling the more complex and abstract concepts such as building resilience and understanding the concepts of life and death. This is detailed in the individual introductions that precede each Article.

The first book looked at the early years of childhood demonstrating how Social Stories can describe all aspects of daily life. These Stories were written for my son but all had been successfully used with other children too, after individual adaptations had been made. In the second book, I addressed the school and college years. I showed how I also used Social Stories *reactively,* responding to situations he had already found uncomfortable and confusing in school and college. Choosing topics that were frequently requested I hoped that parents and teaching staff might be able to use these to prepare other children *proactively* for different situations in school life so that they were more knowledgeable about, and therefore more comfortable in, each situation. The third book addressed developing resilience in the young adult on the autism spectrum, looking at realistic optimism and positive thinking, the preparation of a plan B and the processes of positive self-reflection and positive self-talk.

This fourth book looks at the adult years following on from education. I have selected for inclusion subjects that we worked on together that seemed particularly useful for the practicalities of adult life, and this has necessarily meant that some topics are not addressed in this book.

The social context of an apprenticeship, a job interview and a health check-up are usually similar although rarely identical each time they are experienced. I can be relatively confident that others will experience these contexts in a similar way to my son. This means that sharing these Articles may be helpful for others.

When writing Social Stories or Articles around the topic of relationships, an author must be extremely careful to be respectful of the wishes and needs of the individual audience they are writing for. There is huge diversity in the friendship and relationship needs of young people on the autism spectrum. Some desire relationships, sexual or platonic, others find the reciprocity required in a relationship a burden and prefer to be more solitary. The topic of relationships can be effectively explored using Social Articles; however, describing the thoughts and feelings of others within this context has to be done with extreme care to be *accurate* and this requires a knowledge of each person involved and an understanding of where the relationship is within a timeframe of development. If applied generically, there may be considerable confusion and frustration. This topic therefore contains specific and intensely personal work and for this reason it is not included.

The first chapter in this book addresses the different perspective of the adult on the autism spectrum. Without a good understanding of the autistic perspective it is difficult to identify what information may be missing and therefore what should be written about in a Social Story or Article. Chapter 2 introduces Social Stories and their more adult form, Social Articles, describing how they came to be, what they are and how they can help adults on the autism spectrum. Chapter 3 addresses the difficult time spent in the search for a job – making sense of constructing a curriculum vitae (CV) and attending interviews. The fourth chapter looks at various situations within the workplace. The fifth chapter addresses looking after physical health, with the sixth looking at maintaining mental health. Over the past few years there has been growing concern for both the mental and physical health in young people on the autism spectrum. In this section I hope to share information for my son and others to help keep physical and mental health as robust as possible into the future. The seventh and final chapter begins preparation for the inevitable bereavements that occur in life as an adult by deepening the understanding of life story, life and death.

I have been writing Social Stories and Articles for students, both male and female, for many years but I have only written for one person consistently across his lifespan and that is my son.

He has given his permission to publish these and so as a result there is a predominance of Articles for men as opposed to women within this collection. I am aware that many more girls and women are now being identified as matching an autistic profile and many of these diagnoses are happening in young adult life. I find myself these days writing more and more for girls and women at their request. There is a distinct difference in how autism presents between men and women; however, the underlying difficulty in reading context, particularly implied context, both external and internal, is common to both men and women. Because Social Stories or Articles are written for *individuals*, young or old, of any gender, to describe both the internal and external context of life, this approach can be effectively used for all. Therefore, throughout the introductions and Articles wherever the pronoun 'he' is used it is synonymous with 'she'.

In choosing person first or condition first descriptions of autism I have used 'person on the autism spectrum' in preference to 'autistic person' because this is my son's personal choice. The word 'autism' used throughout is a synonym for 'autism spectrum condition'.

These Articles will be most helpful for adults requiring support, and sometimes substantial support (Level 2) to access the workplace through an apprenticeship, work experience or straight from school or college. Many neurotypical adults may also benefit from some of the Articles.

Each Article has an introduction that sets the scene, then considers the different perception and processing of the adult on the autism spectrum within that scenario. This leads to the information that may be missing for him. A Social Article follows that may have been written for my son, or another young adult, demonstrating how this information is then presented in an accessible way.

The Articles included here share information that may seem 'obvious' and repetitive to neurotypical readers. This information may also be familiar to some on the autism spectrum who have experienced a similar situation multiple times and have consciously learned responses that work within it. The 'obvious' may be required information for some. Repetition may be comforting and predictable for those on the autism spectrum. The purpose of these Articles is to share information when first read, but also to provide a concrete, accessible resource of reference for the future. When faced with an upcoming situation again, like an interview, appraisal or annual health check, the young person can refer back to the relevant Article. This brings more clarity and predictability to the situation and therefore reduces anticipatory anxiety.

Readers will have their own unique person in mind as they read through or dip into this book. That person will not match my son or the others I have written for, because every single person is of course different in their level of understanding, life experience, sensory difficulties, age, insight, need and situation. A Social Story or Article is written for the individual. That is one of the joys of using this unique technique – it is a strategy that exactly matches the young person and it grows up along with the child into adulthood. Social Stories grow up into Social Articles. And if the understanding of the person with autism remains at a younger level, it matches that too, albeit perhaps in a more adult format.

I cannot hope to have included Articles that will be exactly what your young person needs, nor am I trying to do so. In order to write your own Articles, you will need to be trained in the technique first, then after carefully gathering information about your young person's understanding, you will be able to write one specifically for him or her. I hope this book will inspire you to do so. Meanwhile, the introductions will guide you to consider that very important and valid alternative perspective of the people you care for, young or old. As a result, I hope that you may understand them a little better and write Social Articles to guide them throughout adulthood and into old age.

CHAPTER 1

Understanding the Perspective of Adults on the Autism Spectrum

People on the autism spectrum have many attributes and qualities in common that are valued and respected by those who know and love them. They are usually courageous and loyal friends, honest to a fault with a strong sense of right and wrong, straightforward and straight talking, non-manipulative, funny, kind, creative, innovative and inspiring people. Many of these qualities are attributable to the unique way the autistic brain perceives the world, but there are also challenges that come along with this autistic perception in this predominantly non-autistic world.

How people understand the world around them is governed by how the brain processes the vast amount of information streaming in constantly through the senses. People on the autism spectrum (autistic people) process this information in a different way to people who are not on the spectrum (non-autistic or neurotypical people). As a result, they have a different perspective on life from neurotypical people and their responses to situations may therefore seem unexpected, unusual and sometimes even challenging to neurotypicals. Families and professionals frequently note that strategies that usually help neurotypical adults frequently fail for those who are on the autism spectrum. This may lead to the person mistakenly being labelled as non-compliant or defiant. It is important to realise that this unique perspective of the world is as valid to the person as the neurotypical perspective is to a neurotypical, it is not a 'choice' he has made – he cannot choose to perceive in a different way. In a predominantly neurotypical world, life can be very tough for those with an autistic perspective. Frequent negative social interactions and negative social experiences can lead to low self-esteem, increased anxiety and social isolation, which can have a negative impact on mental health.

There are three main validated theories that explain the processes involved in social understanding. Having a grasp of these helps us understand how different the perspective may be if these processes are working differently. The theories are called central coherence (Frith, 2003), theory of mind (Baron-Cohen, 1995) and executive function (Goldberg *et al.*, 2005; Pennington and Ozonoff, 1996). More recently, a fourth theory has been proposed by Dr Peter Vermeulen called context blindness (Vermeulen, 2012). This theory unifies the other theories and in addition suggests an explanation of the other features of autism not completely addressed by them, namely the sensory and literal language difficulties.

Context sensitivity and central coherence

Neurotypicals are inherently context sensitive and have strong central coherence. This means they are able to put together the socially relevant clues in a situation in order to make social sense of it. To do this, the neurotypical brain instantly identifies the 'gist' or context of a situation. This context then focuses the brain only on the details that are socially relevant to that context, in preference to any other details present, in order to make social sense of the new or changing situation (Vermeulen, 2012). All that is not socially relevant is faded into the background. Information is then drawn from previous similar experiences and contexts stored in memory. This instantly helps with the current situation, identifying whether it is safe or dangerous, and importantly allowing prediction of what may happen next. Being able to predict what may happen next enables the choice of safe and effective responses to suit the situation. This all happens subconsciously, innately and intuitively.

In contrast, people on the autism spectrum, despite being able to notice tiny details and changes around them, do not always recognise and use the context. Without a context guiding them to the relevant social clues, they focus instead on details that may be socially irrelevant, but which are particularly interesting for them. They may be described as being 'context blind' and having lower central coherence as a result (Vermeulen, 2012). They are missing crucial social information. This results in a lack of awareness of the *sort* of social situation they are currently in and consequently they are less likely to choose a safe and effective response. Instead, a response may be chosen that is related to the details they have focused on, and this may seem out of place and unexpected to those neurotypicals around them.

People on the autism spectrum require time to consciously work out the context, time that is not always available in the quick to and fro of a rapidly changing social interaction or situation. Similarly, they may have difficulty making social sense of the clues involved in facial expressions, tone of voice and body language of other people. This may contribute to a difficulty in discerning what emotion the other person may be currently experiencing.

As a consequence of this difficulty with reading and using context, change becomes frightening and disturbing and may result in huge anxiety. In order to relieve this anxiety, they may strive to control the people and objects in the environment and keep everything the same – the way that is understood and familiar. They may feel reassured by structure and ritual, being soothed by repetitive activities like watching the same video clip over and over – perhaps the only time they can accurately predict what is coming next. Seeking predictable responses in their interactions with others is comforting and reassuring. A few may even seek a negative response because of this need for predictability.

Responses to negative initiation of interactions are, after all, much more predictable, and usually much more rapid, than responses to positive ones, which can be very variable.

On the positive side, the phenomenal focus of the autistic mind may in part be due to this context blindness, as being less distracted by the social context and the details relevant to it allows a deeper focus on interesting detail.

How this understanding of context changes with time will be unique to every individual and will depend to a certain extent on learning experiences, support and the presence and degree of any additional learning disability. Over time, with multiple learned experiences of a context and with sufficient work done on generalisation, a more comfortable and accurate understanding of context and its common variables can be achieved for some. For others, context that is explicit is not problematic at all, but implicit context remains confusing and will always be so.

As young people move out of education and are no longer exposed to compulsory subjects, lessons, assemblies and sports they do naturally have a greater autonomy over their life. This can initially be a great relief but at the same time may narrow the field of experience dramatically, particularly if the young adult spends long periods of time alone at home. If they are in work, life may stabilise out into two main basic contexts – home and work, with regular visits to leisure places added in. Adults on the autism spectrum are likely to visit the same leisure places over and over and these too may become more familiar over time. As some social competence develops it is easy for others to assume that all new situations can be managed competently and comfortably by the adult. This may be a mistake. Asking the adult if they would like support in new situations is only respectful and should continue.

If work is found which suits the strengths of the individual it may bring a well-ordered purposeful life along with it. Being familiar in the context of the workplace and being knowledgeable about the regular changes that occur there may allow a more comfortable confidence to develop. The rules of the workplace as they apply to the individual within his niche may be consciously learned over time. Colleagues within the workplace may be of varied ages and experience, which brings a mixed set of life skills and, it is hoped, more acceptance and tolerance of difference. As colleagues within the workplace get to know the individual better, friendships may develop.

But this is not the picture for all. The workplace may be a place of continual change and a source of great stress for those who cannot read and use context rapidly and accurately. The continual conscious effort to do so can take a huge toll on emotional well-being over time.

For others, work may be and often is elusive. There is a minefield to tread, working through the maze of job application, CV writing and interviews. There is a great need for support at this stage. This book will address some of the information that may be helpful and gives examples of how this may be done with Social Articles.

Theory of mind

In addition to immediately grasping the context of a situation, neurotypicals are also able to be continually aware of what another person may be thinking, feeling, knowing or believing. This is often referred to as having theory of mind, and a delay or impairment in this process is a common feature to all those on the autism spectrum. Having this ability to be aware of another person's internal context while also understanding the current context of the situation allows a person to know that he may be upsetting, annoying or boring someone else and stimulates him to stop what he is doing, change topic or move away. This keeps him safe and effective in interactions with other people. Without this ability functioning intuitively a person on the autism spectrum may simply not have other people's thoughts and feelings in mind during his interactions with others. He may continue with a conversation, for example, without taking turns to listen, oblivious to the other person's upset or boredom, or he may state a fact about another person's appearance or performance that may be hurtful. This can make it a struggle to make and keep friendships. Lacking mindfulness of what other people might know may also prevent him asking for clarification or help, which means he may remain confused and become more anxious as a result.

Over time as the young person ages, there may be development in theory of mind to differing levels. It will, however, always be a conscious process, rather than an intuitive one. This will inevitably make it slower and more tiring work. Tracking other people's thoughts and predicting their responses in a one-to-one social situation may be manageable, but when another person or two enters the conversation it may become uncomfortable and bewildering. This means friendships between neurotypicals and those on the autism spectrum may continue to be difficult to maintain. However, friendships between those on the autism spectrum may flourish and this needs to be considered and facilitated whenever possible.

The friendship group for a person on the autism spectrum may be large or limited. For some it may be non-existent. Some have a strong desire to have friends or a partner and others find the reciprocal demands of friendship burdensome and prefer to lead a more solitary existence. It is important that neurotypicals do not enforce their ideas of friendship on those on the spectrum but explore and facilitate the needs of the individual. A young adult may be as content seeing one friend every month as a neurotypical may be seeing a friend every day. There really is no 'right' way! Respect for different needs is important here. I have always aimed to help my son develop the skills he needs to interact safely and effectively when he wishes to do so, and then allowed him free choice of how often and when.

Fortunately, some young adults find online contacts who share their interests or even their diagnosis and this can bring a welcome feeling of belonging at long last. However, the internet also may bring many dangers to this group of young adults, who may misread unfriendly intentions of others as friendly, so vigilance by those who care for and love them is needed.

Executive function

Air traffic control resides in the control tower of an airport. Here close attention is paid to the time management, prioritisation, sequencing and planning of the take-off and landing of all the aircraft. If there is an unexpected hitch to a landing, a new plan must be very rapidly formulated for that aircraft by the control tower staff. Aeroplanes are never allowed to take off or land just on impulse. This keeps the airport safe and effective each day and in all weathers.

In a very similar way, neurotypical executive function, which resides in the frontal lobe of the brain, works as a control tower. Executive function manages the thoughts, words and actions sent out by using impulse control, time management, prioritisation, sequencing and planning. When executive function is operating less effectively, which may be the case in young people on the autism spectrum, the ability to control impulses, manage time, prioritise, sequence and plan may be impaired. For young adults already experiencing a world where they cannot reliably predict what will be said or might happen next, being impaired in how they sequence and plan their way through the social world adds to the confusion.

As young adults enter adulthood, executive function may continue to be a significant problem and lead to difficulties within the workplace, which may be a cause of great frustration. Talent may be obscured by lack of adherence to workplace procedure, for example. Those who support a young person on the autism spectrum may need to continue executive function support, putting in place techniques that help the adult improve their own organisation using concrete visual guides.

Language

Neurotypicals can instantly read the context of speech so know when to take a phrase literally and when not to. People on the autism spectrum may not accurately read the context of speech, and therefore do not always understand the intended meaning and this may often lead to a negative outcome for them. Neurotypicals around them may seem to never mean what they say and this can be both incredibly frustrating and increasingly isolating.

People on the autism spectrum may also struggle to make sense of a negative command. A negative command requires the listener to recognise and use the context in order to make a good guess about what the speaker may be *wanting* or *expecting* when they issue this negative command in this situation. This is a task our young people are less able to do well quickly due to both a lack of context sensitivity and a different theory of mind. As a result of their non-compliance with a command, they may then be unfairly judged. People on the autism spectrum need information and directions to be in the positive in order to quickly and accurately understand the intended meaning. Simply rephrasing negative instructions into positive information can change a person's responses, for example instead of using a negative command such as 'Don't overheat the shredder', which relies on implied but unsaid information to allow the shredder to cool down, an instruction using positive information will be much more clearly understood, such as, 'The shredder overheats quickly – allow it to cool down every 15 minutes.' Positive language remains an important need into adulthood to prevent confusion.

In terms of understanding figurative language, over time some adults learn the most commonly used examples and know not to be confused or frightened by them any more. However, how they use these sayings may not always be contextually accurate.

A young person on the autism spectrum may both perceive and experience a great deal more negativity in their lives than their neurotypical peers and, as a result, have a particularly negative outlook on life. It is only fair that this group of young people have access to all this missing social information presented to them in a completely accessible way and this is where Social Stories™ and Articles can really help.

CHAPTER 2

What is a Social Story™ or Article and How Can it Help?

Carol Gray originally devised and developed the Social Story™ approach in 1991 in Michigan, USA. She was working as an autism consultant advising staff about students on the autism spectrum who were included in mainstream education. A couple of schools on her caseload were struggling with the unusual and unexpected responses two particular students were displaying in certain social situations. Despite many attempts to change the students' responses, neither one seemed able to stop or change what was deemed by staff to be an 'undesirable' response.

Carol spent time observing the students within the situations and then patiently and respectfully explored *their* perspective of the situation. She discovered, to her surprise, that assumptions that the students understood what to do and why and were simply refusing to comply were faulty. They were actually missing key social information, without which the demands simply made no sense to them. She discovered that when she carefully described the sequence of the situation and the rationale of the responses of other people, both students were capable of responding in the same way as their neurotypical peers and in fact chose to do so (Gray and Garrand, 1993).

This led to the very first Social Stories™. More detailed descriptions of how these came about can be found on Carol Gray's website at www.carolgraysocialstories.com.

Carol immediately began to write Social Stories for many others on her caseload and had equal success. She began to observe that how this missing social information was presented seemed also to be critical to the effectiveness and safety of the Story. Ten guidelines were subsequently developed for writing Stories. These guidelines have been revised and refined over the years in line with research and experience. They are now called the ten Criteria. Following these Criteria is crucial because they prevent the author from naturally straying into the pitfall of observing an unusual response and then writing a Social Story from only a neurotypical perspective. This is a common mistake and is rarely if ever accurate or effective.

Today, writing a Social Story is therefore a defined *process* which must begin with a considered and careful effort to gather information from the person and the situation in order to discover what social information may be missing for that person. It requires the author to patiently and respectfully explore the perspective of the person on the autism spectrum. To do this successfully, the author has to first abandon any assumptions he has about what might be the reason motivating the response. As a neurotypical, his assumptions are likely to be different to an autistic perspective and more often than not incorrect.

The information gathered may be about any context, skill, achievement or concept in life. The ten Criteria guide the author to not only finding this information, and therefore the specific topic for the Story, but also to actually writing and illustrating the Story. They guide the choice of content, vocabulary, format, tone and accuracy that will make it more accessible for its reader, the 'audience'. They also guide the author in how to actually put the Story into practice. These Criteria maintain the patient and reassuring quality to the Story that sets it apart from just social instructions, social narratives, social rules or scripts. An authentic Social Story will provide a 'learning experience that is descriptive, meaningful, and physically, socially and emotionally safe for the child, adolescent or adult with autism' (Gray, 2015, pp.xxx–xxxii). A guide to the Criteria can be found in Carol Gray's book *The New Social Story Book* (2015) or on her website.

A Social Story patiently and respectfully provides the missing social information by describing the relevant clues in life, building and clarifying the *context* of a situation and creating a comforting sense of predictability. It shares other people's thoughts, feelings and experiences and links these to their reactions and expectations, explaining their behaviour. It does so in language that is positive, accurate, and pitched at the exact cognitive level of the adult and therefore accessible to them. It works hard to engage the adult by considering their choice of interests and may include illustrations to highlight the content of the Story. The result is a uniquely meaningful, patient, non-judgemental, respectful and reassuring description of life, written to ensure the person has all the information necessary to make a safe and effective social response in that situation. Sometimes, but not always, a Social Story™ includes a gentle coaching sentence that suggests an alternative effective response in that situation.

Illustrations in a Social Story are as important as the text. The drawings I use are mostly taken from the Comic Strip Conversations (see page 38) my son and I would usually have before writing the Story. Illustration within a Social Story must be chosen carefully to be literally accurate; in other words the information must be clear from the picture without any contextual understanding being required. No distracting background detail is included. For each child, adolescent or adult that I write a Social Story for, I have to identify the best way to illustrate the text for the individual. Sometimes no illustrations are required. Occasionally more intellectually gifted people find illustrations in a Social Article patronising. However, if illustrations are adapted for their level of understanding this can aid both comprehension and recall, because the visual image is usually so powerful for many on the autism spectrum. Sometimes graphs, bar charts and tables are preferable. Whether to include illustrations or not is dependent entirely on the person the Story or Article is written for and also on the topic.

Many people only reach for a Social Story when they encounter a social response that is considered unusual, usually after other strategies have been unhelpful. I have written a large number of Stories in response to an action that demonstrated a misunderstanding or frustration in this way, for both my son and many others over the years. In my experience as a Social Stories trainer, once the missing information has been identified, and the Story or Article shared, in nine times out of ten the unusual response disappears as a direct result of the sharing of information and improved social understanding.

However, to just use this approach to target specific difficulties for the person wastes another valuable and important use of the approach. Social Stories can be used to describe life *proactively* across the lifespan. Since first learning this technique in 1997 I have been continually writing Social Stories for my son, who was diagnosed as being on the autism spectrum when he was two years old. Each Story or Article I write builds on the last, continually developing concepts, eventually becoming a truly unique description of life delivered in a crafted and meaningful way for him.

Using them throughout his childhood has built a phenomenal trust between us. Mark is confident that I can and will find a translation to bring clarity and predictability to any confusion. This confidence and trust has allowed a continued engagement with the strategy as he has grown and developed into an adult. I have written them through nursery into primary education, first in an autism specialist unit and then in primary mainstream. I continued through secondary education and into college. I am still writing them for him today, 23 years later, as he makes his way as an adult in the workplace.

The format of the Stories has changed as he has grown older and naturally developed different skills, cognition and interests. Initially the Stories during his early childhood were predominantly pictures with three short simple sentences written below them. He was not reading, so these words were written so that whoever read the Story to him would always read the same words, bringing a reassuring predictability to the Story. All the words were carefully chosen according to the Criteria, as indeed were the pictures. As he grew older and developed more language, the Stories changed too, with more words, a wider vocabulary and longer sentences.

Over time the narrative moved from being only in the first-person voice to the third-person voice with occasional first-person sentences, to predominantly third-person voice. Occasionally today when writing for a specific topic that he is wishing to discuss in the first person, for example answering interview questions, the Story or Article may have more first-person sentences within it.

Eventually, as Mark became a young adult, the font both reduced in size and changed in type from Comic Sans to Times New Roman. Times New Roman is the font used in literature and research articles and is usually identified as a more adult font. It carries a certain weight of authority, which my son felt to be more grown up.

The format of the text in the early days used to be one column then changed to two columns, like a printed article, in the later years. Each page was printed on A4 size paper.

As the format has changed so has the title from 'Social Stories' in childhood to 'Junior Articles' in adolescence to 'Social Articles' in adulthood. This change of title demonstrated that the strategy was growing up with him.

As young people today read most of their information online, and the article format of two columns is less often seen in this medium – a single column format with a more modern font may be more engaging for some adults today. The format should be chosen to suit the young person's reading font preference as an adult.

Being curious about what interests another person is always a demonstration of respect for their opinion. Interests are also an invaluable source of vocabulary and imagery that can really help connection and comprehension when explaining challenging concepts or tasks in a Social Story or Article. For this reason, as the audience's interests change the Stories and Articles reference to them must change accordingly. This continual adaptation is critical if engagement with the strategy is to last, out of respect for the individual.

Fifty per cent of all Social Stories and Articles written for a child or adult should recognise and applaud their achievements, qualities and talents. Neurotypicals are aware when people around them are pleased with their performance. This information is often obscured from the person on the autism spectrum. Just as information about what others are thinking in specific social situations is shared within a Social Story, so should the positive thoughts others have about the individual. When authors write 50 per cent of their Stories about the positive attributes and achievements of the audience, they are regularly focusing on what the person is currently doing well. This continually adjusts the author's perspective on the abilities of the person on the autism spectrum. For the person on the autism spectrum, recording these positive skills concretely in an Article makes a resource that adjusts his perspective of himself and can be referred to again and again to build self-esteem and confidence. Certificates and letters of praise may also be attached to a Social Article to enhance positive points made within the Article.

During his years in education my son had a 'Positive Comments' notebook. This recorded verbatim the positive comments of others about him, with a date, time and place (much like a *Star Trek* log). These comments were powerful in adolescence because they came from people outside the home and were not just a demonstration of the love of a family member. As he became an adult, I continued to collect these comments in an adult 'Positive Comment File'. The comments added to this file were from the adult world of work, for example the assessors on his apprenticeship, his employers in the workplace, his fencing coach, his dog trainer. This continues to be an important resource that he often refers to when his self-confidence dips.

During my years of writing I have noticed that Social Stories and Articles work in three important and significant ways on both the author of the Stories and the audience they are written for. First, they *translate* the apparently senseless and illogical words and actions of neurotypicals in the social world, and in doing so they release the audience from the limitations that come with continual social confusion. This enables the wonderful qualities and skills of a person on the autism spectrum to shine through.

Second, and also very importantly, Social Stories *train* neurotypical authors to repeatedly examine their own rhetoric and actions – looking at the illogical way we sometimes talk and act. They train us to question ourselves, 'Why on earth do I ask it like that?' 'What do I really mean?' 'What is the reason I feel more comfortable when people respond like this…?' and 'How can I translate this for a person on the autism spectrum?' This constant re-evaluation of the world as it might be experienced from an alternative perspective changes the way an author communicates and acts. Third, the continual gathering of information from all those involved and collaboration with the team around the person, including parents and professionals, to support the Story has a positive effect on the author too: 'Indeed, the increasing popularity of Social Stories may be explained not only by effects they can have on the audience but also the effects they can have on the authors' (Ali and Frederickson, 2006).

Comic Strip Conversations

A Comic Strip Conversation (CSC) is a technique developed by Carol Gray to explore and share perspectives with a child or adult on the autism spectrum (Gray, 1994). To carry out this 'drawing conversation' all that is required are paper, pens, privacy and two people, one neurotypical and one on the autism spectrum. Its purpose is to provide mutual understanding of each other's perspective. The conversation has a topic, usually a recent situation or interaction, which was either problematic, or deserves applause and recognition.

The conversation identifies where the event took place, which people were present, recalling what was said by whom, and in what order. People are represented by stick men drawings, drawn initially by both parties, but eventually predominantly by the person on the autism spectrum. The order in which the event happened is supported by open, unassuming guide questions such as, 'Where were you?' 'Who else was there?' 'What happened next?' 'What did you say?' 'What did others say?' and so on. These questions are initially required to help recall events in the socially relevant sequence.

Spoken words that are normally transient are written inside speech bubbles and this allows the reader time to examine them and think about them, time that is not available within social interactions. The thoughts or intentions of others are also written inside thought bubbles. Guessing the thoughts or intentions of others may be difficult for the person on the autism spectrum and giving him time to examine his interpretation of another person's thoughts and words is very valuable. His perspective sometimes reveals a completely unexpected interpretation of the motivation or thoughts of other people. This opens up an opportunity for the neurotypical to first acknowledge his perspective as valid and then respectfully draw and write an alternative suggestion. Frequently, the person then comes to his own conclusion that this may explain the outcome, and this develops his understanding of the frequently baffling neurotypical perspective.

The CSC may then go on to explore alternative safe and effective social responses and outcomes. Colour may be used according to a colour chart chosen by the person on the autism spectrum. The colours identify the feelings behind words or thoughts and are used just in the speech and thought bubbles. An example might be green for 'friendly' and red for 'unfriendly'. The information gained from a CSC frequently leads directly to a Social Story as it reveals the important social information that may be missing. Being able to offer an alternative perspective on a situation through this technique can explain what subsequently happened in the situation without apportioning blame or judging the young person's perception as wrong or invalid. This supports one of the underlying philosophies of the Social Story approach – total respect for the *valid but different* perspective of the person on the autism spectrum.

CHAPTER 3

The Search for a Job

Introduction: What is an apprenticeship?

An apprenticeship is a very practical and useful way of helping a young person on the autism spectrum into the often-elusive workplace. However, when introduced it is very important that it is done so in literal, positive and concrete language so that the young person fully understands the *nature* of an apprenticeship. An apprenticeship is a blend of college learning and assessment combined with practical hands on skills in the actual workplace. The time the apprentice spends in the workplace and while studying at college is also paid. This is a new experience for many young people and allows the whole topic of money management to be revisited and implemented practically.

It is also a change, a change of type of learning, environment, people, place and purpose. Changes nearly always need to be supported with clear instruction, often using visual strategies. Visits to the workplace with introductions to the people in the workplace before starting can reassure the young person and reduce anxiety. These visits also allow an assessment of the sensory environment and this may lead to adaptations to improve the comfort of the apprentice, which can influence the success of the apprenticeship.

The structure of learning on the job and the payment rate need to be explained and the purpose of the apprenticeship needs to be clearly understood. If the fact that a job is not guaranteed is not explicitly described at the start, there may be confusion, frustration and disappointment at the end. Qualifications can be gained, which may be of use in the job hunt, but most importantly an apprenticeship is an opportunity to learn skills and discover whether the job suits the young person's strengths. At the same time, it is an opportunity for the employer to learn about the apprentice's strengths and character and how these fit within the workplace.

Employers are often keen to increase diversity within the workplace and welcome our young people but feel anxious about whether they can provide an environment that is comfortable for them. Getting to know and understand the young person over time may reassure them. The young person's skills may impress and his unique perspective on life may add a refreshing and beneficial change to the whole workplace environment. As a result, any unusual and unexpected social responses may be more understood and accepted.

If there is not a vacancy at the end of the apprenticeship it may be forthcoming at some time in the future, so all is not lost. At the very least, the employer will be able to provide a reference that is of value because he has taken time to really get to know the apprentice in a work-based environment, and the apprentice will have additional qualifications and experience to take with him.

The following Social Article describes this information. It was written after I had conducted research into how the scheme would work for Mark. We regularly reviewed the Article during the apprenticeship to remind him of the temporary nature of the placement and the potential outcome.

What is an apprenticeship?

A person who joins an apprenticeship is called an apprentice. The purpose of an apprenticeship is to train an apprentice in the workplace to have the skills and qualifications needed for that particular job.

An apprentice usually goes to the workplace four days a week and goes to college to study one day a week. The work is usually paid at a low rate because it is training. An apprenticeship usually lasts about a year. There are different levels of apprenticeship and different levels of qualification attached to each apprenticeship.

Applying for an apprenticeship is like applying for a job. There is usually an application form to fill in and a curriculum vitae (CV) to submit. If selected for an interview, there is usually an interview to pass.

An apprenticeship is a good opportunity to find out what it is like to work in that job. It is a good opportunity for the employer to learn about the qualities and skills of the young adult too.

Sometimes an apprentice may discover he likes the job and sometimes he may discover he dislikes the job. Sometimes the employer may decide his skills match the workplace and job. Sometimes the employer may decide his skills may be better used in another job. This is all useful information to discover.

Sometimes at the end of the apprenticeship there may be a job for the apprentice to start. Sometimes there may not be a job available. Occasionally, a job may become available later, after the apprentice has finished.

The apprentice usually learns useful skills during the apprenticeship and may gain a qualification. He will also learn what it is like to work in that job. The apprentice may use the employer as a reference for other job applications. This is how apprenticeships work.

Introduction: Words used in a job hunt / What is a job specification? / What is a CV?

The search for a job may be a long and challenging task. A great deal of patience and perseverance is required. During this time, it is easy to become disheartened and to doubt one's own self-worth. I believe that it is important therefore to be careful to keep self-esteem as optimal as possible for young people, and some kind of daily and weekly routine may help. Being involved in a regular sport helps with physical fitness, and mental well-being, and takes the young adult out of solitude for an afternoon or evening (see pages 120–123). Volunteering once a week for a cause that the young person is interested in, whether it is the local steam railway preservation group, the wildlife volunteer group or a charity shop for animal welfare, helps give a feeling of contribution and purpose and is also useful for the CV. The library, often recognised as a place of sanctuary to many young people on the spectrum during school years, can also provide a place to do job searches, browse books or use the internet and is a minimally social place outside the home. Providing each week with some kind of regular structure such as: Monday – library; Wednesday – volunteering; Friday – sport may be reassuring. Embedding some sort of self-timetabling for choice of activities on free days in between may help prevent the negative effects of excessive solitude (see page 120). Of course, solitude is necessary for repair and regulation and may be an increased requirement after any kind of interview, and should be recognised and respected.

In between these activities there is a need to hunt for the right sort of job, prepare a CV and fill in those important application forms. What type of job is most suited for a person on the autism spectrum is not described here because there are several excellent books on this topic and the choice must be individually based. However, there are general points that are common sense. It is clear that a job must match as far as is possible the young person's strengths and therefore due care in selection is necessary. If a job can be found that plays to his strengths *and* includes his interests it is much more likely that he will perform well both in interview and in the workplace. Consideration of the sensory environment is critical here and can often be the significant factor that leads to failure in the workplace. Being aware of the likely environment, from background research, before applying therefore avoids wasting time, effort and self-esteem.

Explaining what a CV is, its purpose and how to put one together using Social Stories™/Articles is very important for a young person on the autism spectrum for several reasons. First, a CV is pivotal to accessing voluntary or paid employment. Having some kind of purposeful employment is crucial to positivity, resilience and mental health for all people (Department for Work and Pensions, 2006). Second, there is a lot of advice about composing a CV both online and in books, but it is rarely explained in concrete, positive and literal language, so there may be lots of misunderstandings about what it is and what it should contain.

Third, because our young people often struggle to hold in mind the opinions, wants and wishes of other people, due to their different theory of mind, they may find it difficult to craft a CV to suit a potential employer's viewpoint and needs, and therefore they may need some neurotypical perspective here to guide them to do so more effectively.

The Latin translation of curriculum vitae (CV) means 'course of life'. Most definitions of a CV describe it as an account of education, professional experience and further qualifications for a prospective employer. The important words here are *'for a prospective employer'*. This is the perspective that needs to be shared.

It is essential that the young person himself is central to the process of writing his CV, developing an understanding of the purpose and thinking behind it. Being able to do this is an important life skill to develop. A neurotypical family member, support worker or friend can help. He or she knows the young person's strengths, and with the help of theory of mind can 'see' what the employer is looking for within the job specification and highlight this to the young person.

Being able to look back on one's life story and retell it in a sequence that does best justice to achievements requires good autobiographical memory. Organisational skills are needed to find certificates and evidence, and social understanding is required to know what not to include and what to highlight. These skills may all be a struggle to some people on the autism spectrum.

When I was helping my son to compose his CV we read the job specification together and then highlighted the talents, skills and qualities required with a highlighter pen. We then looked through his 'Achievements' file containing his qualifications and certificates and noted these down. I had kept an up-to-date 'Positive Comments' journal recording positive compliments paid to Mark by anyone outside his immediate family over the years (Timmins, 2017a, p.37). This was in the format of a *Star Trek* log with the date, time, name and title of the person and the exact quote they had made. Looking at this together we copied down any words that had been mentioned more than once, such as 'focus', 'enthusiasm', 'commitment', 'follows the rules' and 'polite'.

We also looked at a collection of Social Stories™ around 'Challenges Overcome' I had written for him as he was growing up. These described challenges like trying a new food, sport or game, getting through a 'long day' at college (Timmins, 2017a) or answering the phone on work experience, and we briefly noted the title of each challenge overcome and how he had accomplished it.

We then talked together about his hobbies and interests and wrote down what each one involved and what he had specifically learned from doing them. At the end of all this work we had a lot of information that described his talents, skills and qualities. We could then use this in a CV in the best way possible to match what the employer was looking for. The information was particularly meaningful because it came from facts from his life and other people's compliments, not from his mother's heart! It was a very positive afternoon and we both felt incredibly proud of his many achievements, his courage and perseverance in overcoming challenges and his unique talents and abilities.

As I had written Stories and Articles for Mark over many years, we had a lot of resources to tap into. I realise that this may not be the case for many others; however, spending some time writing down the talents, skills and qualities that the young person has is still possible for anyone who knows and cares for him. Asking others who know the person how they would describe his qualities can give a broader insight. Trying to highlight those that match the job specification is also possible with help, even without these lifetime resources. Taking time to talk about the hobbies and interests can lead to a short or long list of skills required to take part in the hobbies or the skills gained from doing the hobbies.

Sometimes this takes a flexibility of thought on the part of the neurotypical person. Abandoning their neurotypical assumptions and judgements first is helpful. A young person may game for long periods online, and this may not seem a worthwhile hobby to discuss on a CV. However, he may be achieving a 'leadership' status within his game and having to organise and balance his team's suggestions for next moves is developing leadership skills. Mark took Japanese evening classes for two years. This at first sight might not seem helpful in the office workplace but it took initiative, motivation and persistence to learn a difficult language, and commitment to attend every week. These are all skills that are valuable in any workplace.

Presenting all life achievements, challenges overcome and special interests in a CV opens the young person up to the pain of further rejection if the application is unsuccessful. This is true for all young people but neurotypicals are more likely to have a supportive friendship group, many of whom have also experienced rejection in their pursuit of a job, and their support can help put rejection into perspective, allowing self-esteem to rebuild. Without this, after numerous fruitless job applications, the young person on the autism spectrum may begin to feel worthless. So there is a need to prepare a 'plan B' in case of rejection (Timmins, 2017b). People who have executive function difficulties may struggle to formulate a plan B. For all the many applications we sent off, and in fact for all our plans in life, Mark and I had always agreed on the next step if plan A was unsuccessful – our plan B. Having a plan B in mind helps alleviate the catastrophic confusion that may occur when plan A fails and the young person is suddenly gazing into an abyss of uncertainty. Plan B, although definitely 'sub-optimal', is at least familiar.

The negative thinking of 'I am not good enough for that job' also needs to be carefully, and consistently, turned into the mindset of being involved in a search for the right job *for him*. If he was unsuccessful in getting the job, then *that job* did not make the grade *for him*. We are crossing that particular job off the list and getting closer to a more enjoyable and suitable job.

The first short Social Article here establishes the terminology used around applying for a job, attending an interview and getting the job. This defines the vocabulary which will be used in the following Articles. The second included here describes what a job specification is and why it is helpful to read it. The third Article focuses on the basics of what the purpose of a CV is, covering what an employer does not know and needs to know from the CV, and the importance of matching skills to the job requirements. It goes on to describe how the details that are supplied need to be relevant to the job described and reminds the young person that someone who they trust may be able to help. These are very simple but important concepts to grasp and understand fully before completing any application form or composing a CV and this information may not otherwise be available for that young person.

For Mark, a template of two different CVs was attached to the Article so it was accessible and ready for adaptation for future job applications, refreshing the information that had already been shared. A copy of his latest CV was also attached. In this way, the Social Article was developing into a 'go to' reference for future applications. These attachments are not included here.

Before even tackling the subject of writing a CV or filling in an application form, I first established why I was qualified to advise on the subject, as unidentified opinion is not acceptable in a Social Article. Here is what we discussed and agreed about my opinion before we started:

> Mum has been a young adult and a mature adult. During her time as a young adult she has applied for many jobs and attended many interviews. She has been successful at some and unsuccessful at others. These experiences have taught her valuable lessons about what to do in these situations. This means that Mum's advice may help in applying for jobs.

All opinion that could be backed up by reference to a relevant research publication was attached to each Article. This made Social Articles for my son more adult, proven and accessible and matched his enthusiasm for proof. However, I was always careful to ensure the research I was attaching shared information that was positive in nature – there would be no point in writing a Social Article in a patient positive reassuring way only to attach a negative reference to it. Sometimes a relevant and supportive quotation from the research article was sufficient. The entire resource needs to be respectful of the young person it is written for.

Words used in a job hunt

When a person applies for a job he may be called an 'applicant'. Once selected for interview he may be called an 'applicant' or a 'candidate' for the job.

When being interviewed by an interviewer he may be called an 'applicant', a 'candidate' or an 'interviewee'.

In an interview, there may be one interviewer but usually there is more than one interviewer. When there is more than one the interviewers may be called an 'interview panel'.

In these Articles, the person applying for a job and being interviewed is called the 'applicant'. In these Articles, the successful applicant in the workplace is called the 'employee'.

What is a job specification?

Usually the skills and qualities required for a job are written down in a document called a 'job specification'. This document is usually in the information sent to an applicant.

This is a useful document because it tells the applicant what skills and qualities the employer is looking for.

The applicant may then choose to write about the skills and qualities he has that match the job specification on his CV. This shows the employer that his talents and abilities may match those required for the job.

Sometimes this is easy to do, sometimes it is tricky. When this is tricky, my team will help me.

What is a CV?

To apply for a job the applicant is usually asked to send a CV. CV is short for curriculum vitae. This is a Latin term which means 'details about a life'.

Sometimes the employer knows the applicant from work experience or an apprenticeship. Most times the employer does not know about the applicant's life.

The CV tells him details about the applicant's life. These details usually include information about the skills, talents, qualifications, experience and achievements of the applicant. The employer needs these details to discover if they match what he is needing in an employee.

It is important that the CV contains details of the applicant's life that are relevant to the job he is applying for. Too many details in a CV may distract the employer from seeing the true suitability of the applicant for the job.

For this reason, it may help to ask a trusted friend or mentor which of my talents and skills will be suited to the job description. Many people ask someone they know and trust to read their CV and give them advice on how it may be improved.

Templates for different format CVs can be found online on this link ...[1]

A copy of my last CV and two different CV templates are attached here.

I may choose one of these or another one to use as a template for my next CV.

---

[1]   Add current link here.

Introduction: What is an interview?

The purpose of an interview is to meet the applicant 'in the flesh' to find out more about him and decide whether he will fit well within the workplace and team. The interview searches for qualities that do not appear on a CV. The interviewer assesses whether a person appears professional, how he responds to questions, and how approachable he is, because it is the interviewer's job to work out how clients, and other employees, might interact with this individual.

Interview skills need to be practised in order to do well at an interview. This is true for all people, autistic and neurotypical. There is a need to be aware of the impression we make on others and how our words can impact on other people's perception of us. We also need to be able to think quickly about what the interviewer may be thinking when he asks a question. A person on the autism spectrum needs much more time to consciously think all of this through. This time is frequently not allowed for in interviews, although once the need is understood many interviewers are happy to allow extra time. Our young adults need all this information about interviews to be shared with them. Employers also need information to be shared with them about the many strengths of an autistic employee, and his needs within an interview or in the workplace.

The purpose of the following chapter is to help optimise a young adult's performance within an interview and the workplace. This can be done by sharing information about the way things are likely to happen and the reasons behind them using Social Articles.

Before any interview takes place, I recommend that a professional speaks to the employer on the applicant's behalf. This is, of course, a personal choice and should absolutely only be done if the young adult understands and gives his full permission. I have, however, on several occasions observed that if autism has not been mentioned on the application form or CV, the interviewer will inevitably notice unusual and unexpected responses during the interview and may attribute neurotypical intention or motivation to these responses, coming to the mistaken conclusion that the applicant may be rude or disengaged, which is untrue and not in the applicant's best interests.

If a person is going to speak on behalf of the adult to the employer, he or she should know the individual well, and know their strengths as well as their needs. It is important not to give a generic talk on autism as much of it may not be relevant to the individual concerned and may confuse the picture. How the information is given is also important; for example, informing an employer that an employee may have a meltdown when exposed to change is likely to worry the employer, particularly where there is frequent change in the work setting. However, letting the employer know that adequate and concrete warning of change is helpful and prevents overwhelming anxiety for the employee, giving examples of how this can be done, empowers the employer, is more respectful of the employee and is eminently doable.

The person chosen should be able to provide back-up information and support, with at the very least the ability to signpost to support in order to reassure the employer. During my son's transition from special school to mainstream, the special school headmaster offered this service to the head of the mainstream school. This reassurance underpinned the transition. It was provided again to the office manager when he started in the workplace. I also offered to give Mark's employer, with my son's written permission, advice on any concerns that might arise within the workplace. This access to information reassures the employer that there are people willing to help him get it right for the employee. There are also numerous agencies that are happy to advise employers about autism in the workplace and mentor those within the workplace.

The following Social Article was written to describe what an interview is, what its purpose is, what the terminology means, and what may be expected to happen. It touches on the first greeting and when and where to sit down and on what. A few years ago,

I was asked to help write a Story for a young woman who did not accurately read the social context of the interview room and subsequently sat on the wrong side of the table. The interviewers were perplexed to find her sitting beside them and she was mortified when she subsequently realised her mistake. This type of social difficulty can be simply avoided by sharing social information on who is using the table, and where the interviewer and applicants' seats are likely to be. I did a lot of work drawing many different ways an interview room may be set out so that Mark learned what key features to look for, for example the interviewers usually sit together and usually have a table. Information like this brings a sense of predictability to the situation, which reduces background anxiety. When he returned from an interview I would draw under his direction how the room was arranged, adding this to the collection.

It is important to explain that sometimes the job may not suit the applicant and that this is actually okay. We learned this when Mark was interviewed for a retail job. This followed on from a two-week work experience placement within the store and a presentation to the manager which all went well. However, despite a reasonable interview he was not given the job. Initially he was very upset by this, but subsequently when he secured a job in an office environment, which was a much better match of his skills, he realised that it was in fact a lucky escape! We frequently reflect together that the first job *did not match his skills* and how glad we are that he wasn't given a place there.

The sensory environment of a workplace needs consideration before applying for a job. Think about, for example, the office environment for someone who has auditory hypersensitivity and a need for regular structure and familiarity: an open plan, hot-desking office is unlikely to be comfortable, and a noisy reception front desk in a busy doctor's surgery is also less likely to be a successful work environment. A quiet back office, however, is much more comfortable and much more likely to work well.

What is an interview?

An interview is a conversation between an interviewer and the applicant in which the interviewer usually asks questions and the applicant usually answers the questions.

Sometimes there is opportunity for the applicant to ask questions. This is usually at the end of the interview. Sometimes the applicant asks for clarification during an interview, and this is okay. Most of the time in an interview it is the interviewer asking the questions.

There may be one interviewer or more than one interviewer. Sometimes an interview involves a task for the applicant to do. If this is going to happen the applicant will usually be told in the information sent to them before the interview.

An interview usually lasts a short time, around 10–15 minutes. Sometimes an interview may be longer.

Usually the applicant is invited to sit opposite the interviewer/s.

Sometimes there is a table in the interview room. This is usually for the interviewers so they can write notes. The interviewers' chairs may be close to this table. The applicant's chair is usually opposite the interviewer/s and further away from the table. Sometimes there is not a table.

When the applicant is called into the interview room an interviewer usually greets them. It is generally expected that the applicant greets the interviewer too. Sometimes this is tricky to do when anxious but practising saying, 'Good morning' or 'Good afternoon' with a smile is a good, friendly way to start.

Sometimes the interviewer extends his hand for a handshake. It is usually considered friendly and respectful to shake his hand. There will usually be an empty chair opposite the interviewer's chair. This is likely to be the applicant's chair. Many people think it is good manners to wait to be asked to sit before sitting down.

The interviewer will usually ask the applicant to sit down. He may say, 'Please take a seat' or 'Have a seat' or 'Please sit down' or 'Please sit'. All of these comments mean 'Please sit down'. Sometimes the interviewer may just gesture his hand towards a chair. This also means, 'Please sit down'.

Many people feel anxious when having an interview. This is a normal feeling to have. Doing some preparation before an interview may help anxiety and performance.

I have a lot of skills and qualities to offer an employer. I am looking for the right job for me. If the employer feels my skills and qualities match what he wants then the interview will be successful and I will get the job.

If the job does not match my skills and qualities then the job is not the right one for me. I may cross that particular job off the list. This is okay. I am getting closer to a job that matches my skills and qualities. That will be the right job for me!

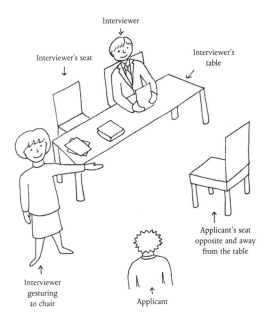

Figure 1: One example of an interview room

Introduction: What is a first impression? / How to dress for an interview

The outward appearance of a person is not an accurate or reliable indication of his or her competency in a job. It is a neurotypical general assumption that if someone looks smart and professional there is a higher likelihood that they may deliver a professional service. As many victims of smartly dressed fraudsters find out, a smart appearance is actually no measure of integrity, honesty or competence. Despite this, a certain standard of tidiness, hygiene and dress is usually expected within an office or business environment. It is commonly believed in our culture to be a sign of self-respect and respect for others in the workplace and engenders confidence in customers and clients. For this reason, adults on the autism spectrum need to know these unwritten, unsaid assumptions so that they can create the best chances they can for themselves in the job market.

Theory of mind is the ability to make good guesses about other people's thoughts, feelings, intentions, knowledge and beliefs and therefore predict what they may say or do. It is often described as delayed or impaired in autism. In the neurotypical brain, theory of mind happens instantly and intuitively but in the autistic brain it is thought to happen in a conscious, thought-out manner and is therefore less quick, and in the rapidly changing world of social interactions it is tiring and inaccurate work.

Being able to take the perceptual perspective of others may also be delayed or impaired in autism. This is the ability to take another person's physical perspective, in other words to be able to accurately guess what another person can see, feel, smell, hear, taste or experience from their vantage point without physically moving to where they are standing. In combination with a difficulty in instantly and accurately being able to imagine the person's thoughts and feelings, this leads the person with autism to being less able to see how others see him, or to know what others may think about him, or to consider at a single point in time that these two may be connected.

Having this different perception brings huge advantages as well as difficulties. Being continually conscious of the social context, what others think, and being wary of looking 'foolish' may inhibit a neurotypical from expressing an opinion or performing on a public stage. Being liberated from the ideas and opinions of others helps some people on the autism spectrum to express their own opinion without inhibition and produce true innovative thought and creative genius.

In the search for work, however, the adult on the autism spectrum needs to be aware of how others may perceive his appearance. In most kinds of business an employer is acutely aware of the impression an employee's appearance may make on meeting a potential customer. To work this out he is using second order theory of mind. This is not intuitively available for the person with autism but it can be consciously arrived at using a Comic Strip Conversation and a subsequent Social Article. The important information to be shared is *why* an employer wants a professional appearance in an employee. When selecting a business to carry out a service, customers may assume that an employee will carry out a standard of customer care equivalent to the standard of care he attributes to his own self-care as evident in his appearance. An employer also is aware that others in the team need to be comfortable working alongside a colleague, so a potential employee's personal hygiene may be noted too.

For those autistic and neurotypical adults who have phenomenal skills that are in high demand, appearance may become less important and different standards of dress tolerated because of the need to engage the exceptional talent. These adults are in the minority, however, and for the majority of all autistic and neurotypical adults looking for work, attention needs to be drawn to how they choose to dress for their interview and subsequently for the workplace.

Over the years, I have had many discussions around appearance and first impressions with my son. His favourite metaphor has always been, 'Don't judge a book by its cover'. I think this is so true for autism! His non-judgemental and respectful attitude to all fellow humans frequently pulls me up sharp to realise that I, like all neurotypicals, am occasionally judgemental about a person's appearance without even being aware I am. This is just one example of how his autistic perspective often challenges and improves my neurotypical perspective of life.

We often confuse our young people by our well-meaning advice around appearance. First, we tell them that it is the inside of a person that matters more than the outside. Then we tell them that it's important to have a smart, clean and tidy outer appearance to make a good first impression on others. Then when out and about we advise them to be careful of strangers, even those with a smart outside appearance and a friendly manner, because they may have malign intentions! All this advice is missing social detail, and context, making it inconsistent, confusing and unhelpful. When advice is inconsistent, confusing or unhelpful it is usually ignored.

As I explored this topic I realised that there was one way to make sense of all the three above statements about appearance, using 'time'. The outside appearance is the *first* impression only. The *second* impression is of the true character of the person, which we cannot immediately see, because it takes *time* to find out about the qualities of a person. With time, the person's qualities are revealed by their words and actions.

With safety in mind there is no time to get to know the qualities of a stranger, and spending time getting to know a stranger may be unsafe, so the advice to remain cautious is logical and sensible. In an interview, however, there is time to ask some questions of the person and try to discover their qualities. It's a short time admittedly but some time is there.

The first impression is just that – a *first* impression. The answers to the questions that follow in an interview form the basis of a *second* impression, which may either confirm a good first impression or even reverse a good first impression. So in an interview, making a good first impression is just the start – the important stuff follows. Importantly, making a good first impression is a *bonus* that helps start the interview positively for the applicant.

The Articles that follow here are: What is a first impression? and How to dress for an interview.

The illustrations are taken from a Comic Strip Conversation (originally stick figure, given more detail here) and are included to emphasise important points from the text.

What is a first impression?

An impression of a person is an idea about that person that is formed quickly without knowledge of the person.

The first thing people notice when they meet someone for the first time is usually the outside appearance of the person. The appearance is how they are dressed and whether they are clean and tidy. This is often called the first impression. The reason it is called a first impression is because it happens first and other impressions follow on.

The outside appearance of a person is less important than the inside character of a person.

The character of a person is the combination of his qualities, for example loyalty, courage, honesty and integrity.

These qualities are invisible when looking at a person from the outside. It takes time to get to know a person's qualities. With time, they are usually revealed by a person's words and actions.

The first impression is just that – a first impression. The person's qualities are the second impression.

Making a good first impression is just a start – the second impression is much more important.

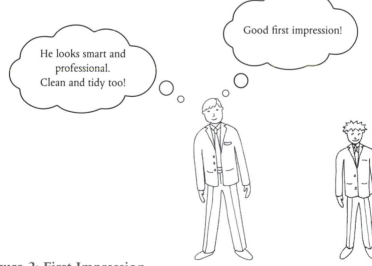

Figure 2: First Impression

How to dress for an interview

When an applicant goes to an interview the first impression he usually makes is by his appearance.

Before anyone speaks, the interviewer usually looks at the applicant's appearance. The interviewer may be thinking whether the applicant will look professional to his clients.

Looking professional may give clients confidence that the applicant will treat them professionally too. This may make them more likely to do business with the company. This is the reason employers look for a professional appearance in an applicant.

Looking professional usually means wearing smart clothes and looking and smelling clean and tidy. This usually makes a good impression on the employer and clients.

The clothes that are most often chosen for interviews by many successful people are usually formal unless the interview information states that casual dress is okay. Formal dress for a man is usually a shirt and tie, smart trousers and a jacket or a suit and tie with clean and polished shoes. When the interview information says dress casual it is still important to look clean and tidy.

Making a good first impression is a bonus that helps start an interview positively for the applicant. Looking smart and professional usually helps make a good first impression.

Yes, he looks professional. I think my clients will think so too!

Figure 3: Professional appearance

Introduction: What does the interviewer know? / What does the interviewer want to find out?

Having a good understanding about what the interviewer is already likely to know helps the young adult have a better idea of how to respond to his questions. The interviewer is likely to know about the job, what skills and qualities are required, and also some details about the applicant from the CV. In order to discover what the applicant might be like to work with and how he would manage both the easy and trickier parts of the job he may ask questions that are looking for this information but may be *asking* something different. The danger here is that in taking the questions literally, the applicant on the autism spectrum may give literal answers and fail to communicate important skills and qualities he has. Preparing the applicant for possible interview questions is therefore crucial if he is going to show himself at his best.

With theory of mind working consciously and not intuitively, he may be less able to work out quickly what the interviewer might mean when he asks a question, and what his intention or motivation for asking that question may be. With difficulty in reading context, both internal (of the interviewer) and external (within the interview situation), the young person may misunderstand the non-verbal clues and make social mistakes. With the huge stress that the interview brings, words may be difficult or even impossible to find. Making preparation for common questions makes the course of the interview more predictable and prepared answers may be easier to find under stress.

My son and I explored about ten questions for every interview, using a Comic Strip Conversation to explore the possible motivation and intention of the interviewer in asking them. This led to a sharing of our different perspectives and more often than not him deciding on an alternative response to his initial one. I then summarised the important information in a Social Article and included an expanded illustration from the CSC.

What does the interviewer know?

The interviewer usually knows about the job the applicant has applied for. He knows what type of work is involved in the job each day. He usually knows the other people on the team. He knows what the easy and tricky parts of the job are likely to be.

Before the interview the interviewer/s will usually have read the applicant's job application and CV. This contains some important information about the applicant, including his experience and his qualifications.

The interviewer usually knows about the job and he may know some details about the applicant. The job of the interviewer is to find out more about the applicant.

Figure 4: What the interviewer knows

What does the interviewer want to find out?

The interviewer usually wants to find out what the applicant is like to work with. He needs to know how the applicant will manage the easy parts of the job and the tricky parts of the job. To find out more the interviewer may ask some questions.

He may ask why an applicant wants this job. He may ask about a challenge the applicant has faced before and how he got through it.

He may ask about an applicant's hobbies. The interviewer may ask these questions in my interview and sometimes he may not. There may be several other questions too.

Being prepared for these questions is helpful. For this reason, many people think about and write down answers to common questions before an interview.

Figure 5: What the interviewer wants to find out

Introduction: How to answer a question about hobbies or interests / How to answer a question about a difficult or challenging situation / How to answer a question about why I want this job

There are many questions that are asked commonly in interviews of all applicants, and the answers scored on a points system so that applicants can be compared in their performance. Addressing four common questions here demonstrates how the strategy of Social Stories™ and Articles can be used to help. Questions of course will vary from job to job but 'Tell me about your hobbies', 'Tell me about a challenging situation you have been in and how you solved it', 'Why do you want this job?' and 'Where do you see yourself in five years' time?' may be asked in many different situations so will be addressed here as examples for reference.

In an interview, the interviewer is trying to find out more about the applicant. Sometimes he may ask the same question in different ways using different words. For example, he may ask any of the following questions:

- What are your hobbies?

- Tell me about your hobbies.

- What do you do in your spare time?

- How do you relax?

- What do you do away from work?

- What do you like to do when not working?

All of these questions are asking about what the applicant chooses to do when not working, i.e. his interests or hobbies. Discussing how all these questions are connected is a really useful exercise. Showing the young adult that what he does 'away from work', or when 'not working', or 'to relax', or in his 'spare time', and for his 'hobbies' are all the same thing can help reduce confusion. I asked my son each question in sequence and asked him to draw or write an answer. When we looked at the answers he could clearly see that all the questions were really asking the same question and had the same answer.

When anxious, many people on the autism spectrum find it reassuring to talk about something that interests them, and once launched on the topic of their hobbies may continue for some time, feeling the benefit of being immersed in their favourite topic. They may not notice the social cues given by the interviewer indicating that he wishes them to stop. They may start to talk about a special interest assuming the interviewer has asked because he wants to find out more about this topic. This, after all is what questions usually are asking. However, questions in an interview context are often not looking for information on a topic but are looking to find out more about the applicant.

A Comic Strip Conversation can help explain what the interviewer's perspective might be, and what he may be thinking when he asks this question about hobbies. It is important and respectful not to argue perception during a CSC but to simply offer an alternative perspective. During a CSC around the question 'What are your hobbies?' Mark said he thought the interviewer wanted to know about fencing, its rules, the different weapons used and the grades of expertise. I was able to offer the alternative perspective that the interviewer may be interested in the skills developed in fencing that could be used in the office environment, such as following rules, politeness and commitment. Once the potential intention of the question was understood he was then keen to do some helpful preparation for this type of question before the interview. Thinking about what skills and qualities his hobbies had developed in him, or were needed to carry out his hobbies, helped him answer the question about his hobbies *and* showcase his qualities and skills at the same time. As Mark concluded, 'My hobbies can tell the interviewer about my strengths!'

Work around this topic involves a lot of focus on what the young adult's qualities and skills are as mentioned earlier. If he knows he has qualities and skills that are valued he will have more confidence in the interview.

For example, my son enjoys both dog training and fencing in his spare time. The skills and qualities that are needed to do these hobbies are also helpful skills to have in the workplace.

Patience and *perseverance* are needed in dog training because sometimes it takes time and a lot of practice to learn a new trick. To be a fencer means he has to *follow rules* each time he fences. He goes to a fencing club once a week and to dog training once a week which shows *commitment* to a club and a trainer. Patience, perseverance, compliance with rules and commitment are all valuable qualities to have in the workplace. An adult on the autism spectrum may need some help with working out how his skills are reflected in his interests and hobbies.

When asked about a challenging or difficult situation the applicant has been in and how he solved it, the interviewer is trying to find out how the applicant deals with frustrating challenges. Demonstrating that with help the young adult can navigate a challenge and gain new skills is one way to answer this question. Comic Strip Conversations really helped here and an enhanced segment of one illustrates this Article.

When asked about why the applicant wants *this* job, the young adult may miss the meaning inferred by stress on the word 'this' and its implication – 'this job *rather than any other job in this field'*. Reading and interpreting inflection is often a struggle for a young adult on the autism spectrum. He needs to know and understand the inferred meaning here so he can answer well. Without this explanation, a literal interpretation of this question may lead to the answer, 'Because I want money for my food and internet' and this will not help him impress the interviewer. So it is important to have some positive evidence for choosing this job, which can be found by doing some straightforward research online before the interview. It may also be sensible to add that the job matches his specific skillset, if indeed it does! Research before applying for a job is always valuable because the applicant may discover that the sensory environment or skillset for the job does not match his needs. Doing thorough research may therefore prevent wasted time, effort and self-esteem.

The following three Articles were written in the first person as they followed work done through Comic Strip Conversations on questions that had already been asked in a practice interview. Sometimes reversion to the first person is needed when more complex understanding is required as it is more easily understood, provided the audience does not perceive this as patronising. The whole CSC is not included in the Article, just exerpts from it, to show concretely the possible thoughts of the interviewer when asking the question. Information about a possible answer is included in the Article. Once reviewed, the illustration was a visual that could be more easily recalled and helped comprehension. Each Article is kept brief to make a single point. All the 'question' Articles would be together in the resource folder as a series.

How to answer a question about hobbies or interests

Sometimes the interviewer may ask the applicant about his hobbies or interests. The interviewer may be trying to find out whether his qualities and skills will match what the job needs.

To answer this question it may help to prepare using two steps:

Step 1

Find out from the job description what qualities and skills are needed for the job.

Step 2

Think about hobbies and what qualities and skills they require or have given the applicant.

Describing hobbies in a way that shows that his qualities and skills match those needed in the job may increase the applicant's chance of success in the interview.

For example, I usually like to do dog training and fencing in my spare time. These are two of my hobbies. The skills and qualities that are needed to do these hobbies are also helpful skills to have in the workplace.

Dog training needs *patience*. A fencer needs to *follow rules*. Going to a fencing club every week for six years shows *commitment*. Patience, following rules and commitment are also helpful qualities to have in the workplace.

Here is one way I decided to answer the question 'Tell me about your hobbies';

'I train my dog Rosie once a week with a dog agility trainer. I need a lot of patience to do this because it takes her a long time to learn a new trick. She enjoys learning and it's fun.

I also enjoy fencing. I like the rules of this sport. I have fenced at a club every week for the last six years, completing all grades.'

I may choose an answer like this or maybe something else. I am learning how to tell the interviewer about my qualities and skills by describing my hobbies.

Figure 6: Tell me about your hobbies

How to answer a question about why I want this job

Sometimes an interviewer may ask me why I want this job.

The interviewer may be wondering why I chose to apply for this job *rather than any other job*. He may want to know how important this job is to me, and if I know anything about the business or service.

It is important to do some research online or visit before an interview to find out some facts about the business or service. Using these facts may help me to answer the question.

The interviewer will usually like to hear some positive reasons for the applicant wanting the job. One example of an answer may be, 'This company is the largest in this town with a great reputation and I would be proud to work here.'

I will try to find and use positive facts about the job in my answer.

Figure 7: Why I want this job

How to answer a question about a difficult or challenging situation

Sometimes an interviewer may ask an applicant to talk about a challenge he has faced and how he overcame it. The interviewer may be wondering if the applicant is able to solve a problem in a positive way and if he will ask for help when needed.

Choosing a challenge that was overcome and led to a new skill is usually a good answer. Sometimes this is easy to think of, sometimes it is tricky. My team can help me choose an example.

One example I have used before is:

'When I worked in … office I carried out office duties. One of those was answering the phone. I find answering the phone stressful. My supervisor helped me by giving me a script to use when answering the phone. She sat beside me while I was learning to use this. Over time I learned to answer the phone comfortably using the script.'

I may use this example or use another example when I answer this question.

Figure 8: A challenge overcome

72

Introduction: How to answer the question, 'Where do you see yourself in five years' time?'

This common interview question absolutely does not mean what it says. When asked this for the first time in a practice interview Mark did not answer despite having many sound plans for his future. The practice interviewer subsequently advised him that he needed to put together a plan for his career or aspirations so that he could answer the question. Not answering at all looked like he lacked motivation and direction to the neurotypical interviewer. When I asked what the question had been I immediately knew he had been confused by it. Later he confirmed with me that he had been thinking the answer might be 'in the mirror' but he also knew this was a ridiculous question in an interview (which demonstrated some contextual awareness) so the question must mean something else that was unclear. Confused by an unclear question, he opted to say nothing and wait for the next question. The practice interviewer immediately assumed a neurotypical motivation for his response – that he did not have any career plans – which was a huge error.

When I suggested an alternative meaning of 'Where do you see yourself in five years' time?' might be 'What do you hope to be doing *in your career* in five years' time?' he could immediately understand and reply with a very sensible answer that showed he had plans, aspirations and was highly motivated. In fact, he had so many plans we needed to try and pare them down to be feasible within the next five years! Eventually he decided on the following possible answer, 'I hope that I may be a senior admin assistant here, having taken and passed the higher-level business and admin exams.'

We explored together how the question might present in a slightly different way and looked at several alternatives. We decided that '…in five years' time' was the phrase to look out for that was linked to 'tell me your career plans for the next five years'. Of course, I knew that the question might still confuse him if asked obscurely.

It was this experience that made me address asking for clarification of a question in an interview (see page 84).

It is sometimes difficult for a person on the autism spectrum to understand the meaning conferred by an additional emphasis, or inflection, on a word. Struggling to read the context and the non-verbal language may leave him confused. Sometimes I use emphasis on a word to imply a level of certainty to a plan; for example, when asked if we were going to a specific place, I answered 'Yes, we *will* try and get there this afternoon.' Verbally emphasising the 'will' implied that we would definitely be doing so. Needing clarification, Mark asked me if the 'will' in this sentence was in regular, bold, italic or bold italic font. Replying that it was in bold italic helped him understand that the likelihood of us getting to the place was strong – I was committed to it. Describing the 'font' of my spoken language is sometimes helpful to clarify my meaning! In this Article, I used the bold oblique font for the words 'in my career' to emphasise them. This Article was written after a practice interview and suggests an effective response for the interview question relevant to the job. When applying for a different job, the Article was of course altered accordingly and this demonstrated the need to adapt answers for different job interviews. Over time and after several interviews, this became a familiar process.

How to answer the question, 'Where do you see yourself in five years' time?'

Sometimes an interviewer may ask the applicant, 'Where do you see yourself in five years' time?' This question is really asking the applicant *what he hopes to be doing in his career* in five years' time. The interviewer may be wondering whether he has a career plan and where the job he is applying for fits in his plans. One answer may be, 'I hope that I will be a senior admin assistant here, having taken and passed the higher-level business and admin exams'. I may use this answer or maybe something else.

Whenever an applicant is asked a question in an interview that is unclear it is okay to ask the interviewer to ask the question in another way.

Figure 9: Five years' time

Introduction: Glancing in an interview

Young adults on the autism spectrum often struggle to make themselves comfortable in the neurotypical world. They may seek resolution of their discomfort themselves, rather than ask others for help or understanding. This may result in an unusual social response which is then wrongly labelled a 'chosen behaviour' by the neurotypical observer. I have learned so much from asking the child or adult the reason for their response. I have also lost count of the many situations I have been in where professionals and parents have assumed a neurotypical intention for an autistic response and have been in error – none more so than in the area of eye contact.

If we take the time to listen to people on the autism spectrum like my son they tell us that eye contact for them is often uncomfortable, unbearable or not useful. This is why many choose to avoid it. They frequently describe that in order to listen rather than looking at the speaker they need to look at a plain or unstimulating surface, like the floor or a wall. For others, it may be that looking at someone's face is pointless because they do not receive useful social information from doing so, or they do not know that others need them to look in order to show they are listening.

The neurotypical assumption, however, is often that when someone is avoiding eye contact it may be because they are not listening, do not wish to listen, are guilty or ashamed, or showing disrespect. Mark, like many other children and adults on the autism spectrum, frequently avoids looking at the area of the face around the eyes, particularly when the person is unfamiliar or there is negative emotion in the air. Once Mark was able to tell me he found eye contact uncomfortable a Social Story™ was written to validate the sensation he was feeling, to acknowledge the difficulty this posed for him, and then find a compromise that was respectful of this, but also shared information on what others need to know. Sharing the Story with teaching staff involved during his school years was a very valuable way of explaining Mark's different perception of the situation and this also helped improve their understanding of his autism.

Looking at a colleague or employer to show attention is an important skill in the workplace. Without this skill, a person may appear to be uninterested and switched off in a world of his own, when in fact he is actively trying to pay full attention. His colleagues from their neurotypical perspective may consider him deliberately rude. It is important therefore, while helping him understand their need to be looked at, that we also help them to understand his different perspective.

Although the original Story started with Mum as the person he was learning to listen to, for school and college this was replaced by the 'teacher' then 'tutor'. This used the original Story as a master copy, a Story Master, from which other Stories, in a similar format, could be made to build generalisation of the skill of listening to different adults in different settings.

While working on interview skills in the hunt for a job, I used the Story again as an Article Master, replacing 'teacher' this time with 'interviewer'.

It is important to realise that although this Article may appear repetitive to some neurotypicals, for some adults the repetitive nature of the format is reassuring and familiar, and in a world where it is hard to predict what is going to happen or what someone is going to say, this feels comforting. For others, however, the repetitive format may appear childish so considerable effort must be taken to individualise the Story or Article for its intended reader. A Social Article should always be written at the exact cognitive level of the reader, with the format, sentence length and vocabulary chosen specifically for the individual. Keeping this in mind at all times helps prevent the adult or child feeling either patronised or challenged by a Story or Article. The following Article keeps to the format of writing in the first person because it matches the format of previous Stories written for Mark on the topic of glancing. The interviewers were both identified to be female prior to the interview, so 'she' is used here as the pronoun referring to them.

Glancing in an interview

When interviewers are talking in an interview it is important that the applicant shows that he is listening. This is because listening to an employer is a valued skill in the workplace.

The interviewers usually know the applicant is listening when he looks at their faces while they are speaking. Some people find looking at faces uncomfortable, especially when the faces are unfamiliar.

To keep comfortable and show the interviewer that he is listening a person may look at the interviewer for just a short time and then look away. In a little while he may look at the interviewer again. Looking for a short time and then looking away from someone's face is called 'glancing'.

I have an interview at about 10am on Monday morning at … Office. There will be two interviewers on my interview panel. One will be the manager, and the other will be the deputy office manager.

Figure 10: Glancing in an interview

When an interviewer is talking to me I will try to glance at her face. Then she will know I am listening and I may feel comfortable. Showing that I am listening by glancing in an interview helps to make a good impression on the interviewer.

Introduction: How to ask for clarification in an interview

Job interviews are stressful for all people. They may be exceptionally stressful for a person on the autism spectrum because they involve a face-to-face social interaction, with verbal and non-verbal communication, during which everything about the interviewee is scrutinised and analysed by the interview panel. An interview may be extremely hard won, and the opportunity to work so important and desperately wanted, which adds to the stress.

Preparation is so important here. Familiarity about the sequence, the process and the likely questions in an interview really helps both neurotypical and autistic adults. All young people should be encouraged to think about common interview questions, write them down and work out a way to answer them so that their talents and qualities can shine through their answers. Before each of the interviews my son was called to, we spent time together considering a series of common questions. Before thinking about answers, we wrote down his talents, skills, achievements and qualifications (see pages 36–37). Then going through each common question I used Comic Strip Conversations to discover what he believed the interviewer might be thinking when asking that particular question. I then shared an alternative perspective of what I guessed the interviewer may be thinking. Our perspectives were different and we learned from each other. When an alternative thought was more logically sound, Mark was very comfortable with changing how he would answer the question. It now made more sense to him. It continually impresses me when I write Social Stories™ and Articles for children and adults on the autism spectrum just how flexible their responses are when supplied with the equal information to their neurotypical peers. Information presented in a respectful and positive way is the key to improving flexibility.

It is important in an interview that the applicant is given sufficient time to think about what the question is asking and then given further time to answer. Providing the person gives their permission, someone from the team supporting him, or someone from an informed organisation involved with autism, can speak to the potential employer about the talents and strengths of this applicant, as well as the differences that might make a formal interview stressful. The requirement for extra time can be raised during this discussion. As a result, the interviewers should allow the applicant longer to answer, and be responsive to any request to clarify a question that is unclear for the applicant.

Having the confidence to ask someone to repeat a question in an interview is difficult. Sometimes instead, the applicant may just not answer and this may give a mistaken impression of uninterest or lack of respect for the interview process. Knowing how to ask for clarification and perhaps practising the line out loud beforehand may help confidence. Showing the employer that when unsure the applicant will ask for clarification and not just 'muddle through' is a good example of how he will cope with uncertainty in the workplace, and that is a positive skill not a negative one.

Prior to writing this article for Mark I made sure he understood what an 'unclear' question was by discussing it with him and listening carefully to his definition and also by referring to a dictionary together. I also ensured that he understood exactly what 'clarification' meant. Mark had developed a very advanced vocabulary by early adulthood but I still always check that his understanding of any words used in a Social Article is sound before I write.

How to ask for clarification in an interview

In an interview, the applicant is usually asked several questions by the interviewer/s. The applicant usually tries to answer these questions.

Some interview questions are easy to understand and answer. Some interview questions are difficult to understand and answer. It may be tricky to know exactly what the interviewer wants to know. These questions are unclear.

When a question is unclear, it is okay to ask the interviewer to make the question clear. This is called asking for clarification.

One way to do this may be to ask, 'I am unsure what the question means. Please can you ask the question another way?'

The interviewer will then usually ask the question in another way. If the question is still unclear it is okay to answer, 'I am still unsure how to answer your question.' The interviewer will then usually move to another question.

Asking for clarification is important because it shows the interviewer that when the applicant is unsure he is able to ask for help. This is a useful skill to have within the workplace.

Figure 11: Asking for clarification in an interview

Introduction: I have an apprenticeship!

After many job applications, many carefully composed CVs and many unsuccessful interviews there will eventually be a successful one. After all the hard work the taste of success will be sweet and should be savoured and celebrated because it has been hard won. After a successful interview, Mark was finally awarded a place on the apprenticeship he wanted. This was a moment to be marked with a positive 'Praise Social Article'. Just as in other Social Articles, the thoughts and feelings of others needed to be shared with him. The following brief, simple and very positive Social Article was written immediately to describe the positive thoughts of the interviewers and the positive feelings of the family about my son's achievement. Of course, a celebration involving pizza and Jaffa Cakes followed.

I have an apprenticeship!

Today I was successful at my apprenticeship interview and have an apprenticeship starting in September! This is a great achievement because there were many other very good people applying from the college who also wanted the apprenticeship.

The practice manager told me that I did an excellent interview, answering all of the questions thoughtfully and intelligently. She said the interview panel think I am an interesting person with a wide variety of fascinating interests, who will be welcomed onto the office team. This combined with my references and academic achievements meant that they both agreed without any doubt that I was the right person for the job!

I feel really proud of myself. Mum and Dad and all the family are proud of me too! We will celebrate this great achievement as a family with a pizza tonight and some Jaffa Cakes!

CHAPTER 4

The Workplace

Introduction: What does being on time mean?

Being on time to work is a valued skill that is often the focus of the yearly appraisal and unfortunately all too often the reason for disciplinary procedures occurring in the workplace. Arriving on time to start work takes planning, self-discipline and good time awareness. Neurotypical people often struggle with these skills and people on the autism spectrum struggle with them too. Being aware of the time and the time remaining until a deadline, such as leaving the house to get to work, can be an issue for those with executive function weaknesses. Our young people have a terrific focus on the task in hand and this, combined with a lack of time awareness and weak planning skills, may result in them being late for both work and leisure activities.

Sometimes the change from home to work causes massive anxiety because the person cannot face the crush of people on public transport in the rush hour. The proximity and noise of a crowd of people causes sensory overload and massive anxiety and naturally leads to avoidance. Flexible working hours allow a more comfortable journey to and from work. Part-time work, which suits the requirement for restorative solitude that many people on the autism spectrum need, also helps relieve anxiety.

For those in jobs with fixed hours, understanding the neurotypical perspective is helpful in order to know the reason why importance is placed on arriving on time. A different theory of mind may lead to simply not holding in mind the thoughts and feelings of other colleagues or the employer. Once this information is shared and consciously thought through it is easier for the young person to comply because it now makes much more sense.

The neurotypical language is full of phrases that are difficult to make sense of without reading both the context of the person saying them, and the context of the situation they are being said in, and 'being on time' may be one of these phrases. There is nothing 'being' about it. It means *arriving* on time. This can be described as a skill which a person can have – the skill of punctuality.

Some years ago, I was asked to help an adult woman on the autism spectrum with intellectual disability who became extremely upset when told that someone 'was late', or alternatively that she 'was late' for an activity. It was clear on talking with her that she had little understanding of the concept of the word 'late'. She was 'Jan'. She was not 'Late'. I could completely understand her frustration in being told she was another person or thing, and then being denied access to an activity which had already started. I wrote the first Article describing with clear visuals that each activity usually had a start time and a finish time. I described that arriving before the start was called 'being early' and arriving after the start time was called 'being late'. Being late meant there was a shorter time in the activity. Other Articles developed the idea of people setting up the activity and looking forward to starting it with her, and their disappointment when they had less time to do the whole activity before the finish time, building in the most positive way the importance of getting there on time to start. It developed into a series of Articles which were very successful. She understood much better what was being said and what was being asked of her. The staff also now understood her reaction and did not attribute it to 'behaviour'. Sharing perspectives with each other in Social Articles led to improved understanding on both sides!

For young adults who do not require such intense support it is still important to inform them of the underlying reasons for being punctual. Describing the perspective of others and how their work may be impacted by a late arrival of a work colleague is required. This information may just not be there for the person on the autism spectrum. The reason we need employees to arrive on time is so that the work process of the office or workplace can happen; for example if an employee is late to sort the mail, other employees may be waiting to act on correspondence and unable to action tasks due on that day. There is a need, however, not to overemphasise this so that anxiety is generated or obsessions triggered around the time of arrival.

As my son approached adulthood and apprenticeship, we discussed punctuality and I wrote a Social Article. Punctuality had already been introduced at a simpler level during the school years so as a topic it was familiar; however, it needed to be put in a workplace context to help generalisation.

The fairness of giving the employer all the hours of work he has paid for is another concept that is covered in this Article.

What does being on time mean?

In an apprenticeship or workplace there is usually a fixed time to start and a fixed time to finish work.

Arriving at the workplace so that the employee is ready to start work at the starting time may be called 'being on time'. Arriving after the starting time may be called 'being late'.

Usually employers notice and are pleased when an employee is good at being on time to start work. Being on time is also called 'being punctual' and is a good work skill to have. Being on time means that others are not waiting for another person to arrive in order to start their work. Being on time usually helps the workplace work well.

Sometimes this start and finish time is moved to make work happen earlier or later in the day or night. This may be called working 'flexible hours' or 'shifts'. When working flexible hours there will usually still be a time when an employee or apprentice will be expected to start and finish their work.

A workplace usually has a finish time. It is important to remain at work until the finish time unless there is an exceptional reason. Exceptional reasons may be one of the following, or may be something else:

- if the employee becomes unwell and is unable to continue work
- if the employee has an appointment or holiday leave during the working day away from the workplace
- if the employee is asked to leave early by their employer.

Employees are paid to do a set number of hours of work and starting work on time and finishing on time usually means the employer is receiving the amount of work he is paying the employee for. Starting and finishing on time means being fair to the employer.

When leaving before the finish time for any reason it is important to tell the line manager or employer. Telling the line manager allows him to reallocate tasks to other people in the office. This way important work tasks get done.

Being on time helps the workplace work well.

Introduction: Teamwork in the workplace / Helping colleagues in the workplace

There are very few jobs available nowadays that are completely solitary. Trawling through the job adverts continually reveals the requirement to be a good communicator, work as a part of a team and be a multi-tasker as well as multi-skilled. Part of getting along in the modern workplace involves teamwork. This is not always welcome news to those on the autism spectrum. Teamwork may be really difficult because it involves continually being aware of other people's contexts in an evolving project context. This is exhausting if not impossible for many young adults and it usually does not play to their strengths.

A good team member contributes the best he can for the team in whatever task he has been given so that the final aim is achieved. To be able to do this a person has to accept the role allotted to him by the team leader, accept that someone else may have been allocated the task that he considers to be his strength, and then take direction, and perhaps constructive criticism, of work in a task he may feel less equipped to do. It can be a tough call.

This Article simply explains what to expect in teamwork in the office environment. This is a good example of a proactive Story or Article written to describe the context so it may be more predictable and comfortable for the person.

Apart from 'teamwork' there is the important skill of being helpful to colleagues in the workplace. This is also fraught with social rules that are unwritten and unseen but important in making friendships. Here the Article proactively raises awareness of others needing the help of the person on the autism spectrum, whether in helping with a particular task such as IT, physically carrying or moving something or even offering a drink to others when making one for oneself. Plenty of time was spent discussing these topics with my son using Comic Strip Conversations in preparation for the workplace. What happened in reality was that he always asked if he could help and frequently offered drinks, but these were often declined. I tested his tea- and coffee-making abilities practically to make sure his skills were up to scratch. We discussed the different possible responses of the staff. We even invented a checklist of how 'brown' the staff might like their drink, with a set of shades to indicate different strengths of tea and coffee printed on a card in his pocket. Eventually, a member of staff told me that his colleagues did not want to put him to the bother, as they valued him and wanted him to have his free time on his breaks! Sometimes neurotypical people are just extraordinarily kind.

This Article includes an example of the work the young person is likely to be asked to do as part of a team. Clearly this was specific to this particular office job. It needs to change for each job the person applies for and must be specific to the job description.

Teamwork in the workplace

Many jobs involve teamwork. Teamwork means people working together to achieve an aim. In the workplace, this involves each person on a team contributing his skills to a project.

An example of teamwork might be when notes are digitalised. To do this involves teamwork. One person sorts the contents of the notes in the correct order, one person moves the sorted notes to the filing cabinet, one person scans the sorted notes onto the computer and files them, and one person shreds the unwanted notes.

Everyone has something that they are good at. Some people are good at IT. Some people are good at communicating with customers. Some people are good at filing things in alphabetical order. Others are good at making things practically, or something else.

Teamwork means that each member of the team works on a project by using the best of their skills. The team leader decides who does each task on the team, and this is okay.

My main skill is IT and I am also good at filing, franking, shredding and photocopying. I may be asked to help the team with any of these tasks. This is okay.

Working as part of a team helps the team achieve its aim.

Helping colleagues in the workplace

Helping colleagues at work is a friendly thing to do and makes the workplace a more comfortable place to be. Sometimes a colleague may need physical help such as carrying a heavy load or moving a heavy item. Another time a colleague may need help with a particular aspect of their job, for example an IT problem.

Before helping a person, it is respectful to ask first, 'May I help you?' This question gives the person the opportunity to say if he or she does not want help. Sometimes a person may want to do something without help, even if it is difficult. When the person does not need help, a good answer may be, 'I am fine but thanks for offering'. This answer gently refuses the offer but importantly also acknowledges the kindness in offering help.

Sometimes it is friendly to offer colleagues a hot or cold drink when making one at coffee break. Asking each person first ensures that the right drink is made and reduces potential waste. Sometimes colleagues will say 'Yes', sometimes colleagues will say 'No, thank you' or 'I'm good' or 'I'm okay, thanks'.

All of these phrases mean they do not want a drink at this time. This is okay, and asking is still a friendly thing to do.

The workplace is usually a friendly place where people try to help each other.

Introduction: Helping colleagues with mistakes

Noticing detail and identifying errors is usually a real strength in people on the autism spectrum. This ability may lead to a career but it may also lead to broken friendships and strain workplace relationships. No one likes to be shown to be in error in front of others. There is a real skill in highlighting and then helping someone to fix a mistake without damaging their self-esteem. Neurotypicals can quickly read the context of the situation and the internal context of the group of people as well as the internal context of the person and adjust what is said to suit all. A neurotypical might decide to say nothing or might tentatively and *quietly* say, 'I hope you don't mind me saying, but I think there may be an error here.' From an autistic perspective, this statement is inaccurate because the error exists – there is no 'think' about it, he 'knows'.

Guiding a person on the autism spectrum to make a socially safe and effective response here is tricky. Finding and then sharing the missing social information is key. Describing the alternative perspective helps. I wrote the following Article for a friend's son, H, who loudly corrected people at work, which was causing resentment among his colleagues. His mother told him to inform the line manager rather than the individual concerned but this only made things worse. When I asked him what he thought the person who committed the error was thinking he replied, 'I made an error. I don't know how to fix it.' I suggested that he may be thinking, 'I made an error. I feel stupid. I need to fix it before anyone notices.'

I went on to discuss with him what the person might think and feel when his error was highlighted to everyone in the office. He replied that the person would be pleased that H had found it and would fix it. He thought the person should be grateful for his intervention and help and he was expecting praise and gratitude. I suggested an alternative possibility could be that the person may be feeling disappointed, uncomfortable and even perhaps a little embarrassed, thinking, 'Now everyone knows I made an error everyone will think I am stupid.' He was interested in this alternative thought and was happy then to work with me to plan an alternative response.

We agreed that making an error was uncomfortable and also agreed that the offer of help was a good and friendly one. We decided that speaking quietly so that others were unaware was a kind thing to do and also that giving the person an opportunity to refuse help was also respectful. A few possible sentences were suggested to do so. One he particularly liked was included as a gentle suggestion, or 'coaching sentence' within the Article.

Apparently, the young man, who was highly talented in accountancy, continued to correct others after the Article but he did so in a *quiet* voice and using the exact words I had suggested. His colleagues felt this was a significant improvement.

Helping colleagues with mistakes

All people make mistakes sometimes. When a person makes a mistake he or she usually feels disappointed and uncomfortable. Sometimes the person may notice and correct the mistake. Sometimes the person may be unaware of the mistake.

In the workplace, it is usually the line manager's job to notice and help with mistakes. The line manager usually does this with office employees in private.

Sometimes an employee may see an error in another colleague's work. The employee may want to help his colleague correct the mistake. It is important to be careful of a colleague's feelings while highlighting or helping with a mistake.

Speaking quietly so others cannot hear and also using words that are helpful and positive is a friendly and respectful thing to do.

If I notice a mistake in someone else's work I will try to speak quietly to them and choose helpful and positive words. One way of doing this is asking in a quiet voice, 'I have noticed a mistake here. Would you like me to help you fix it?'

Sometimes the person will want a colleague's help. Sometimes the person may not want a colleague's help. This is okay.

All people make mistakes sometimes.

Introduction: Keeping colleagues comfortable at work

This Article is included at the request of a few parents and also employment support workers who found this topic to be a common difficulty. Fortunately, it is not a problem that I have had with my son. This may be because I covered personal hygiene proactively years ago before he became a teenager, or it may be just because he loves his baths!

The important information to share here is that within the workplace everyone tries to keep those around them comfortable, as this shows respect for self and others. Good personal hygiene is also a healthy practice that helps prevent skin infections. Information also needs to be included as to how to achieve good personal hygiene. It is, however, still important to gather information from the young person because the reason they may not comply with personal hygiene may not be because they do not know how to do it. The reason may be very surprising to the neurotypical person. I once wrote an Article at the request of a mum for a young man who refused to accept that his body odour was uncomfortable for others because *he himself could not smell it.*

Consequently, the Article included information on how to go about good personal hygiene but importantly also had information about how the position of the nose on the front of the face often meant that it was tricky to smell one's own odour, whether it was a fragrant or a strong smell. However, others moving past with their noses above or behind the person's hair, or at the level of the armpit as in a queue in the cafeteria could smell the body odour very easily. I advised the mum to do some innovative practical work to support this along with reading the Article, and the problem was solved. This young man was happy to comply when he could read and *smell* the rationale!

Keeping colleagues comfortable at work

In the office, colleagues usually sit at an allocated desk to work. Sometimes other colleagues sit nearby at their desks. There are often more than four people working in the same office. Colleagues sometimes walk around the office to carry out their various tasks, walking past other desks on their way.

As colleagues share the same office and work closely together, it is helpful if the office is comfortable for everyone. One way to keep each other feeling comfortable is by having good personal hygiene.

Personal hygiene means keeping the body and hair clean and smelling good. Washing the body and hair each day in the shower or bath and using a deodorant after washing and drying the body is good personal hygiene. This usually keeps the body and hair clean and smelling good. Smelling good makes it comfortable for colleagues to be working alongside and near each other.

Having good personal hygiene is a healthy habit too. The body needs sweat and dirt to be washed away each day so that infections of the skin are avoided.

Having good personal hygiene shows others that the person values the comfort of people around them and values their own body too.

Introduction: Asking for clarification in the workplace

For all young adults, the search to find a job may have been a long and painstaking one with numerous rejections and disappointments along the way. Of course, for some it happens straight away but this is usually an exception to the rule. Once achieved, it is an opportunity the young person on the autism spectrum wants to make the best of. He is usually highly motivated to make it succeed and is prepared to put maximum effort into doing so. Once the daily tasks involved within the job are established and familiar there is comfort in doing the usual things each day. Routine brings clarity and predictability, which is reassuring.

However, inevitably over time new tasks will be asked of the young person and sometimes this may be done in language that is unclear and inaccessible for him. There is a need to ask for clarification of the instruction, or alternatively help with the task. For our young adults starting out in an apprenticeship or the workplace, self-esteem and self-confidence in the neurotypical world may be very low as a result of many previous negative experiences of being misunderstood. A young adult on the autism spectrum will nearly always try to solve problems by himself, without asking others to help. For some this may be a trust issue, or it may simply be because it doesn't occur to him that others may have the information or the motivation to help or even that others expect him to ask if help is needed. For others who want to ask for clarification, the anxiety of the moment may be overwhelming, preventing them from finding the right words to do so. Being mindful of the unspoken thoughts of another person is often a challenge because of theory of mind differences. In a confusing situation being able to consciously think this through may be difficult. Muddling through a task may result in mistakes and wasted time and resources which may have a negative impact on self-esteem.

I always try to ensure that my son or the young person I am writing for knows that when he is unclear what to do in the workplace it is important to ask for help or clarification. He needs to know that more experienced colleagues may have this information and will expect to be asked, and that they can help him. This information fills in any gaps from the different theory of mind processing. Naming two specific people who will be happy to help is a concrete support and giving a script choice of possible ways to ask may be useful too. This proactive information is provided in the following Article to *avoid* a misunderstanding. Practising a phrase, or another of his own choice, out loud outside the workplace makes this more familiar. Within the home environment this can be modelled when family members give each other an unclear instruction.

If the situation arises when a young adult does not ask for help and makes a mistake, they may feel a failure and need reassurance that all people make mistakes and that mistakes happen on the way to learning new skills. This is another topic for a Social Article!

Asking for clarification in the workplace

At work, each employee has tasks to complete. Usually he knows how to do these tasks. Sometimes he may be asked to do another task that he is unfamiliar with. Sometimes it is clear what to do, sometimes it is unclear.

More experienced colleagues may have done the task before and know how to do it. They may be able to help. Asking for clarification from colleagues may help avoid mistakes and may avoid wasting time too.

When something is unclear it may help to think, 'Others might know. Others can help. It's smart to ask.'

One way to ask for help may be to say, 'I am unsure how to do this, please can you help me?' or 'Please can you clarify what I am meant to do?' or maybe something else.

The people who can help in this workplace are Mr T and Mrs R. They will be pleased to help. I will try to ask for help or clarification in the workplace when I am unclear what to do.

Usually asking for clarification from colleagues helps avoid mistakes and avoids wasting time too. Asking for help when unclear what to do is part of being a smart and responsible employee.

Figure 12: It is smart to ask

Introduction: Using earphones in the workplace

Discomfort with loud noise has been a continual difficulty for Mark throughout his life, due to auditory hypersensitivity, as it is for many people on the autism spectrum. Sometimes we have found that using Social Stories™ to explain the purpose of the noise and its likely duration has made the discomfort more meaningful and therefore more tolerable, but has not eliminated the sensory impact for him. Acknowledging the discomfort caused by noise, and gentle direction towards the use of earphones or headphones to diminish the effect of the noise have also been really helpful. As a result of Stories suggesting strategies to keep himself comfortable in noisy situations, Mark has also learned to take his earphones wherever he goes to help him cope with an unexpected noise level.

The noise factor in the workplace was an important consideration when Mark was job hunting as a young adult. Looking for quiet office work he applied for an apprenticeship in office administration within a medical practice and was called for an interview with the practice manager and the deputy manager. As we waited for him to be called to his interview I was struck by the noise levels in this very busy doctors' surgery. There was an unwell child crying, another child throwing a tantrum, electronic 'pings' calling patients to their consultations, general patient chatter, electronic doors opening and closing and the general background noise of people coming and going. Mark was clearly uncomfortable and quickly put in his earphones. It was clear that he would not find working in this front reception area comfortable.

However, he was successful in his interview and was awarded the apprenticeship. The interviewers were clearly impressed with him and wanted to sign him up as soon as possible. We were subsequently very relieved when he was informed that his apprenticeship placement would take place in the back office away from the noisy reception area, which was an ideal environment. However, his duties involved using a very noisy shredder daily and when there was a baby vaccination clinic running next door the babies' shrieks could easily be heard through the office walls, causing him a lot of discomfort. Thankfully the practice manager was committed to making him comfortable in his workplace and listened to our concerns, allowing him to use earphones when using the shredder and during baby vaccination clinics.

Because Mark was so comfortable wearing earphones, gradually over time he began to wear them not just at those times but most of the time. I became concerned that wearing earphones continually could be a safety issue for himself and other office colleagues. It might also mean he would not hear other people's requests. The social side of being included was probably more of a concern for me than him, but equally Mark would not like to appear disengaged or unfriendly, which might be the mistaken assumption of others if he was wearing earphones continually. It became important to share with him information about why it was important to be able to hear what was said to him, and why others might like to speak to him within the office, information he did not have intuitively due to his theory of mind difference.

I initially explored this with a Comic Strip Conversation showing his colleagues' thoughts and words so he had time to look at these thoughts and words in a concrete way. We acknowledged together that some noise was too uncomfortable and we made a plan of when and where earphones could be reasonably used during his average day. We agreed that using them before work, while travelling to and from work and in the staffroom on breaks were reasonable times to use them. Using them in the staffroom allowed him to recalibrate himself before going back to his job. The pictures from the CSC were incorporated into the text.

This Article was immediately successful and Mark continues to use his earphones now only when using the shredder and during vaccination clinics. This has allowed him to be involved with conversations with his colleagues and as result workplace friendships have developed. A simple Article with a huge impact!

Using earphones in the workplace

The back office at … Medical Centre is a busy office with lots of staff and many pieces of office equipment. One piece of equipment is the paper shredder and it is part of a junior administration assistant's role to do the paper shredding. This is an important task because it keeps patients' details confidential. The paper shredder makes a lot of noise when it is switched on and used. This noise is made by the motor and stops when the machine is switched off.

This noise may be uncomfortable for some employees. It is okay for an employee to use earphones when operating the paper shredder to keep comfortable.

Next door to the back office is the room in which the baby vaccination clinics are held. Babies usually cry when they have vaccinations.

The babies usually stop crying when their parent comforts them. This noise may be uncomfortable for some employees. It is okay for an employee to use earphones during baby vaccination clinics to keep comfortable.

Office colleagues work together as part of an office team and often need to ask each other questions, share information or request help. Occasionally an office colleague may need to alert another colleague to a danger.

Having conversations with colleagues during the working day is part of being a friendly team member. So for many work and safety reasons it is helpful to be able to hear other colleagues while working in the office.

For these reasons, it is important to use earphones in the office only when using noisy equipment, during baby vaccination clinics and when there is sudden unexpected noise.

There are places where it is okay to use earphones during the day. It is okay to use them at home before work and while travelling to and from work. It is also okay to use them in the staff rest room during coffee and lunch breaks.

Introduction: How to request holiday leave

Holiday leave is an entitlement for all employees. However, in the workplace staff continuity is important for the success of the business or service. If more than a critical number of employees are away from work on leave, on training, or off sick there will not be sufficient staff present to do the work. So there is a need to have holiday leave staggered in timing throughout the year. This rationale does not have to be explained to many neurotypicals because they can easily assume the perspective of the employer and the business using their highly effective and intuitive theory of mind. But for some neurotypical and autistic people there may be a need to explain the reasons for requesting holiday leave, awaiting approval before booking anything, and accepting that if a holiday leave request is put in at a late date it might be reasonably refused. Sharing information about other people's perspectives and the procedures with a Social Article is helpful. This Article became part of a 'Work Resource' file of Social Articles. Requesting annual leave often only comes around once a year so having the information to refer to again is important.

When a person starts work there is usually an induction day when the new employees are familiarised with the policies and procedures of the workplace, and this can vary from being informal to quite formal instruction. It is likely that the disciplinary procedures, health and safety procedures, grievance procedures and sick day policy and pay will be among the information discussed. Along with all of this will be how to request holiday leave. The information will be given verbally and usually in hard copy too. Sometimes, however, there is a problem with the accessibility of the information for adults on the autism spectrum. To begin with, the terminology 'holiday leave' may not have been used before. The term holiday or annual leave usually means time away from work, paid for by the employer, for the employee to use in whatever way he wishes to. An employee may be expected to 'go on holiday' but he may not wish to travel but prefer instead to stay at home and do his chosen activities or interests, and this is perfectly acceptable. Lots of people choose to stay at home during holiday leave for many different reasons.

In order to ensure my son had all this information we talked about it in depth, checking that he had a clear understanding of the employer's perspective, and also knew his rights and how to request leave. The following Article was written as a summary of our discussion together and I hope will serve as an accessible resource for his future employment.

How to request holiday leave

The term 'holiday' or 'annual leave' or 'holiday leave' usually means time away from work paid for by the employer. Usually each employee has a fixed number of days they can have as holiday each year. An employee may choose to go away from home or stay at home during holiday leave. Many people choose to stay at home during annual leave for many different reasons and this is okay.

In the workplace, each employee has a job to do. Each job helps to make the whole business work well. Usually employees work hard at their job. Each employee is entitled to holiday to relax and have fun. So that the workplace can work well it is important that only one or two employees are away from work at any one time.

Employees may be away from the workplace for many reasons. They may be on holiday leave, sick leave, bereavement leave, maternity/paternity leave, at a different site, at a doctor's appointment or on a training course. They may have another reason for being away from the workplace.

For this reason, it is important to let my employer know my holiday dates so that he can check how many other colleagues are away at the same time. If there are enough staff in the workplace during my holiday dates the employer will usually confirm that it is okay to take my holiday.

Each workplace usually has a system for requesting holiday leave. Some have a Human Resources department (HR for short). HR departments usually have a person who looks at all holiday leave requests and confirms whether the dates requested are okay to have. There may be a specific form to fill in with the dates for holiday leave. This may be on paper or online.

When starting in a new workplace there is usually an induction day when the new employee is shown all the procedures of the workplace. Information about how to request leave is usually given at this time. My line manager Mrs … can help me find the name of the person who deals with holiday leave in my workplace.

Sometimes a holiday leave request will be approved, sometimes a holiday leave request may be refused. Giving in holiday leave requests early helps the chances of being allowed to take the holiday at that time. Usually an employer likes to receive the dates more than a month before the holiday.

Having a break from work usually helps employees feel refreshed and ready to work again when they come back to work. I will try to remember to request my annual leave early and use my holiday leave to do something I enjoy.

Introduction: What to do when feeling unwell at work

A young adult on the autism spectrum may have received support during school years from his learning support assistant at school and parents and family at home. When he is unwell, this 'team' would look after him and ensure that he was safely picked up from the school and looked after at home. In the workplace, with no one allocated in an assistant role, he may be unsure of how to manage the situation when feeling unwell.

Knowing what to do is important because when unwell most people's thinking skills deteriorate, whether they are autistic or neurotypical. In addition, because planning skills may be less strong in a person on the autism spectrum, having a clear plan of what to do can really help. Understanding what the correct procedure is, and importantly the reasons for it, improves recall of the plan when stressed by illness.

Because of the differences in theory of mind a young adult may not think of the need to inform his line manager of how he feels and just leave the workplace to return home without telling anyone. This may have serious repercussions. First, it may be unsafe for him to travel or be alone unwell at home, and second, the work he may have been allocated in the workplace will not be done. Informing the line manager and a member of the support team ensures that he is safe and that the work can be reprioritised and reallocated.

This is a short and simple Article that gently suggests a script of how to ask to go home. The last three paragraphs are in the first person narrative as it was reflecting on a specific course of action to put in place when unwell. It was used proactively to provide this important information. It was easy to recall and once it had been used in the workplace successfully there no longer was any reason to feel anxious about being unwell there.

What to do when feeling unwell at work

Most of the time at work employees feel well and able to do their work. Sometimes an employee may feel unwell at work. Sometimes it is possible to carry on working while unwell, but sometimes it is difficult to continue working.

When this happens, it is important to tell the line manager or employer and request permission to go home. Telling the line manager allows him to reallocate tasks to other people in the office. This way important work tasks get done. This is okay.

When this happens I may use a phrase like, 'Mr D, I am feeling unwell and need to go home', or I may use another phrase.

Telling someone on my team that I need to go home from work is very important too. I may need help getting home or managing at home while feeling unwell, and they can help me.

Telling my line manager and someone on my team know that I feel unwell helps me be safe and helps get my work done.

Introduction: What is an appraisal?

Most jobs have some sort of appraisal system, which is an opportunity for the employer and employee to meet and reflect on the parts of the job that are going well and reflect also on the parts that are not going so well. The employee can tell the employer how he perceives his performance in the workplace and the employer tells the employee how he perceives the performance. Both are sharing perspectives of the same thing but from their differing standpoints. Some of the perspectives will be the same, some may differ. The objective is to improve things for both parties using constructive motivation, working together to find solutions and to further both the professional development of the employee and the efficiency of the workplace.

An employee on the autism spectrum may have a different perception of the workplace environment from the employer and other neurotypical employees. He may have sensory differences that cause him discomfort or distress that affect his ability to work. He may struggle with change and the flexibility this requires in the workplace. He may also follow instructions literally, not reading an implied context, and this too may affect his work. Social situations and interactions may be difficult for him to read and understand. Most importantly, in an appraisal he may have difficulty in seeing his performance from another's point of view. There is a need to share perspectives to understand each other.

Explaining the purpose of an appraisal and then preparing a young adult beforehand may help his understanding of his employer's concerns and get the most from an appraisal. Explaining an alternative autistic perspective to the employer may require outside help in the form of a support person or mentor, who has experience and knowledge in autism. This person may also need to attend the appraisal if the adult wishes them to.

Appraisal reports, if positive, are a wonderful concrete affirmation of the person, which may be attached to the Article in order to boost self-esteem. When the person comes to reread it for the next annual appraisal not only are they relieved by the familiarity of the information about what is likely to happen, they are also reminded of a previous good outcome, which builds confidence.

What is an appraisal?

In most jobs there is usually an appraisal of each employee. An appraisal is a meeting between the employer and the employee in which they talk about the employee's performance in the job over the last year. An appraisal may happen several times a year or only once a year.

The purpose of the appraisal is to praise good work and identify any problems or difficulties early and then find solutions for these problems together. An appraisal also may encourage employees to learn new skills through taking up training opportunities.

An appointment date and time to meet the employer/s is usually sent to the employee before the appraisal.

During an appraisal the employer asks the employee what he has enjoyed in his work and what he has found challenging in the work. This is a chance to let the employer know how the job could be made more comfortable or more accessible.

The employer also tells the employee what he is pleased with, and what he thinks could be improved in the employee's work.

The employer may talk about the time keeping, appearance, professional manner, teamwork and flexibility of the employee. The employer may talk about other topics too.

At the end of an appraisal a plan is usually agreed to solve any difficulties and help the employee work more comfortably and to the best of his ability. A report of the appraisal is usually sent to the employee. A copy of last year's appraisal is attached here.

Introduction: Moving from unsettled to settled in the workplace / Meerkats have unsettled times too

Our thoughts have a critical effect on our emotions and choice of behaviour. This is the basis of all cognitive behavioural therapy. Many neurotypicals experience thinking as an internal conversation, talking to ourselves, which we usually carry out silently. We describe this as self-talk. Some young people on the autism spectrum may also use self-talk but they often talk out loud to themselves. Self-talk can be positive or negative and therefore has the ability to help or hinder our self-confidence when we face a new or challenging situation.

For our young adults, change usually causes huge anxiety. Small changes that can be taken in a neurotypical's stride can completely terrify them. Even returning to a familiar day-to-day situation after a weekend, short break or holiday may result in overwhelming anxiety. Positive self-talk can be learned and practised in this situation, and in many others, as a method of self-calming, allowing the young person to refocus on the facts and knowledge they have about a situation to regain confidence and reduce anxiety. In addition, the use of portable calming strategies that have been identified as working for the young person can reduce anxiety and improve confidence. Together these two strategies can make him feel more comfortable and more able to cope. Both of these strategies need to be practised when he is in a comfortable place before putting them into action outside the home.

Mark experienced several episodes of feeling unsettled when he returned to his apprenticeship placement or subsequent workplace after a break. We chose the word 'unsettled' to portray what he was feeling in this situation because it was accurate, as he was neither anxious nor calm. It also allowed us to describe a return to a 'settled' state. I had a drawing conversation with him about where he worked and having explored that there were no new factors within the workplace that required describing or explaining, we wrote down together several key things he knew about the workplace both from fact and past experience. I then wrote an Article describing how he could move from unsettled to settled again using his calming strategies which had worked for him before in the past. Following this I wrote factual statements, from the information already gathered, for him to *quietly* recite as self-talk when faced with unsettled feelings before going in to work. I also wrote this down on a small card for him to keep in his pocket. This combination of Article and self-talk worked well on this and several other occasions.

Although Mark was, and is, able to use his positive self-talk statements well, it is important to note that I always explore the context of each individual situation he is experiencing anxiety in with him too. This is because a familiar context may change and he may become uneasy about it but be less able to recognise what the new context is, and importantly whether it is safe and friendly or not. He may, like many other young people on the autism spectrum, also become aware of a negative atmosphere but may not have the context sensitivity to truly understand the meaning behind it. So before encouraging him to use his positive self-talk statements, I gather information from the situation, and from both Mark and others, around any changes that may have taken place. A Social Story™ or Article should never be used to make a person endure an unsafe or unfriendly situation.

Linking positive self-talk statements to positive visual images can be really helpful here. Many young people are strong visual thinkers. Temple Grandin, who is a high-functioning autistic professor in animal behaviour says, 'I think in pictures. Words are like a second language to me… When somebody speaks to me his words are instantly translated into pictures' (Grandin, 1996).

I have found that if I can link an abstract concept with a meaningful concrete visual image for the young adult I may be able to engage them in a more meaningful way that can be instantly recalled for future use. What seems to be important for my son and others is that the images chosen are from interests of theirs. For example, in Mark's case I frequently used meerkats or penguins which were, and continue to be, a real interest for him. Meerkats, through their behaviours, are the living embodiment of what it feels like to be highly vigilant and anxious, always on the look-out for change. They also visually demonstrate the comfort of being with family and safe friends where they rapidly relax and drop off to sleep comfortably. Watching the series *Meerkat Manor* on DVD with Mark has given me many opportunities to use characters and situations to explain feelings, emotions and the reactions of others.

The second Article is included here as an example of how I used images of meerkats to improve the understanding of feeling unsettled when a change is happening. It was written early on in Mark's apprenticeship several years ago and is in the Article format in the first person, to suit the need at the time.

Of course, some young adults will not be able to understand analogy and some may find the illustrations and analogy patronising, so each Story/Article must be written at the cognitive level of the individual using constructs that they understand and are comfortable with.

It should be noted that the word 'can' should be used with caution when writing self-talk statements for a person on the autism spectrum. If the skill being described is not currently within the skillset of the person, 'can' should be avoided.

Social Articles need to be monitored from time to time to ensure that they are still valid and accurate for the person. Sometimes a new aspect to an Article needs to be added. For example, recently we noted that my son felt unsettled and 24 hours after initially feeling this way the symptoms of a heavy cold emerged. Thinking back to his childhood I clearly remembered that this was a pattern. His behaviour changed at least 24 hours before an illness became noticeable. We decided together that this important information needed to be added to the Article. Sometimes he feels unsettled just before a cold starts.

Moving from unsettled to settled in the workplace

Sometimes I feel settled at work and sometimes I feel unsettled at work. Many people feel settled some of the time and unsettled some of the time at work.

Thinking about what I know about the workplace may be helpful. My workplace is usually a safe place. The people in my workplace are usually friendly and safe people who like me. I usually know what to do in my job and my boss is usually pleased with my work. When unsure about something at work there are two people I can usually ask for help: ... or ....

I have felt unsettled in my workplace before and become settled again after a short time. I felt unsettled when I came back to work from a long weekend away and from holiday. I used my calming strategies and my self-talk statements to move from feeling unsettled back to settled.

Recently I felt unsettled and my strategies helped only a little bit. Twenty-four hours later I started a cold. When my cold was better I felt settled again. Sometimes I may feel unsettled when starting a cold.

Sometimes when I feel unsettled using my calming strategies helps me feel settled again. Sometimes using my self-talk statements quietly to myself helps too. I am learning to move from unsettled to settled.

I know this place and it is a safe place.
I know the people who work here.
They are friendly and safe people who like me.
I know what to do in my job.
I know what to say in my job.
I know who to ask for help.
I have done this before and
I can try to do it again.

Figure 13: Self-talk statements

Meerkats have unsettled times too

Sometimes meerkats feel settled. Usually meerkats feel settled when everything is happening just as normal and life is going peacefully according to plan.

Sometimes meerkats feel unsettled. Meerkats usually feel unsettled when changes happen within their burrow. Sometimes there is a change of routine. The leader may decide to lead a foraging trip for food at an unexpected time of day. This usually makes the meerkats feel a little unsettled.

They still go foraging for the same length of time. They still go foraging to the same place. They still go with the same group of meerkats.

When the meerkats have foraged at the new time for several days they usually begin to feel settled again. Life soon returns to normal.

In my apprenticeship things are feeling a little unsettled. The hours I am working have moved from the morning to the afternoon. I am still going to be with the same group of people. I am still going to be working in the same place. I am still going to be doing the work I normally do.

Many people and meerkats feel unsettled when there are changes to the routine. When I have worked at the new time for several days I usually begin to feel settled again. Life soon returns to normal.

Life often has times when a person feels unsettled and times when they feel settled again. This is how life happens for all people and all meerkats.

When I feel unsettled I will try to use my self-talk and calming strategies until things feel more settled again. Life will soon return to normal.

——— CHAPTER 5 ———

Maintaining Physical Health

Introduction: Keeping the body and mind healthy with exercise

There is a substantial amount of published research showing the benefit of exercise not only on the body (Pate *et al.*, 1995) but also on the mind (Powers, Asmundson and Smits, 2015). As a result, the World Health Organization (WHO) recommends at least 150 minutes of moderate aerobic exercise each week for adults aged 18–64 in order to improve cardiorespiratory and muscular fitness and bone health, and reduce the risk of non-infectious diseases and depression (World Health Organization, 2011). Exercise is usually safe, inexpensive and portable.

People on the autism spectrum often need and seek out periods of solitude to rebalance and restore their well-being after social activity. As a group, they are more often than not talented in IT and interested in screen-based activities. This may lead to a more solitary and sedentary lifestyle than many of their neurotypical peers. The reduced level of physical activity, combined with unusual dietary patterns, and sometimes medication that causes weight gain, may result in the young adult becoming overweight. Being overweight or obese is recognised as being associated with long-term health problems.

This is of course a problem for many neurotypical young adults too; however, recent research has highlighted an alarming premature mortality in people on the autism spectrum owing to a multitude of medical conditions, which has focused attention on their mental and physical health (Hirvikoski *et al.*, 2016). An explanation for this could be an increased biological vulnerability to disease in this group, or insufficient understanding of autism in health professionals impeding their diagnosis and treatment. It is also certainly true that some struggle to identify symptoms and communicate these with others or seek help for them. While the results of ongoing research into the cause are awaited, there is an urgent need to help our young people develop awareness of their health, seek help early when unwell, and adopt a healthy diet and lifestyle, including exercise.

Getting involved with exercise is often a challenge for many people. Joining a club or gym requires motivation, planning and being social, all of which may be more difficult for the person on the autism spectrum than the neurotypical. School sports have been, more often than not, a negative experience and there is little incentive to continue sport when school is finished – in fact, not having to do it is often a huge relief. Many have difficulty with co-ordination and sensory overload, which makes exercise more challenging and much less enjoyable. Others find the social side of sport uncomfortable. For these and many other valid reasons the person on the autism spectrum may be less likely to take regular exercise.

In order to encourage exercise, working through the channels of the special interest and physical or sensory needs is vitally important. Exercise doesn't need to be taken at a sports club. It can begin with walking the pavement at a regular pace. This is often a chosen self-calming activity for many young people with autism anyway. Listening to a soundtrack taken from a favourite game can make it an extra calming experience. Using an interest, for example in Japanese culture, can lead to taking up Taekwondo or another martial art. My son enjoys fencing and has recently taken up archery, both skills prevalent in olden times and represented in many online games. Tuning in to the individual's sensory requirements may help direct them to a sport that may provide these too; for example if an individual seeks out proprioceptive input, choosing trampolining, weightlifting or swimming might all fulfil those needs. The choice of sport must be a personally suited one. For those who struggle with teamwork, the solitary sports are a better fit, such as cycling, jogging, horse riding, skating, trampolining, weightlifting, swimming, fencing or archery, to name but a few.

Introducing the sport using literal language is important too, and describing realistically what the young person may initially achieve within that sport helps prevent disappointment when they are not immediately successful. Having some concrete and visual guide to progress or improvement in the skill of the sport can encourage engagement, for example badges or certificates for levels of expertise. An understanding of personal best is very important too. Competing against himself with his own targets of personal best results may be more enjoyable than competing against others. We started this with Mark in his childhood using the Social Story™, 'What is my personal best?' but in adulthood it continues to be an effective way of making even competitive sport more comfortable for him. Recording his results against regular opponents, in a personal best score book, allows him to see improvement in his score even when he loses a match (Timmins, 2017b, pp.234–239). Using his personal best strategy allows him to continue in a sports club with all the social benefits that come with that too.

I have frequently found that the actual skills needed for a sport may be better introduced, practised and acquired initially in a one-to-one situation with a coach or trainer. The trainer may need to break down the skills required into achievable steps. Introduction to a sports club is likely to be more successful when the young adult is confident with the basic skills of the sport. Having to learn the skills as part of a group, deal with winning and losing, and be sociable all at the same time is often too much to ask.

I was keen to help Mark to take exercise for his physical and mental health. Once established as a habit I knew it could become a lifetime habit so I produced the World Health Organization's article and we talked about the evidence together. He was already fencing once a week and walking the dog daily. I encouraged him to join a gym and have sessions with a personal trainer to devise a programme that would suit him. He agreed. The Social Article here summarises our discussion, providing information on why doing exercise was a good idea, how it could help anxiety, and goes on to describe the different types of exercise. The scientific evidence in the articles mentioned above was attached to the Article for his further reference.

Keeping the body and mind healthy with exercise

Many scientific studies have shown that exercise is very important to keep the body and mind healthy. The World Health Organization therefore recommends that adults aged 18–64 years take at least 150 minutes of moderate aerobic exercise each week in order to improve cardiorespiratory and muscular fitness and bone health, and reduce the risk of some diseases and depression (WHO, 2011).

Exercise may help anxiety too. Anxiety is internal energy that builds to help the body prepare for a challenge by running or fighting. Exercising the body may help get rid of excess energy and make the body feel better and the mind calmer. Regular exercise usually makes the heart beat slower.

There are many kinds of exercise. Some people exercise by running along the pavements, others just walk quickly. Some go to the gym where they exercise on machines, some go to the swimming pool and swim laps. Some people join sports clubs and do a favourite sport like fencing or football. Some people have coaches to help them exercise well and improve their fitness, while others exercise alone.

Exercise may be done in the home too, for example running up and down stairs, hoovering, and cleaning and mopping. Exercise may be done outside the home, for example walking the dog, skateboarding, sweeping the drive, and raking up leaves. There are lots of ways to do exercise.

Some sports are social, many are solitary. It's okay to choose a sport that is comfortable for me. I enjoy fencing and I fence once or twice a week at a fencing club. I usually go to the gym once a week to train with my coach. My coach knows what exercise programme I need and how to alter it to build my fitness. I usually walk my dog every day too. Exercise is also good for my dog.

Exercise is important to keep the body and mind healthy.

Introduction: Keeping the body healthy with a varied diet

Sensory dysregulation plays a significant part in the limited diet that is often encountered in young people on the autism spectrum. Some children are hyposensitive to a sensation, others are hypersensitive and some have a mix of hypo- and hypersensitivities to various sensations. The perception of taste and texture may be amplified, dimmed or distorted. Experiencing what others describe as 'delicious' as uncomfortable or even painful must be confusing and distressing for a child. Of course, the solution for the child is to only trust foods that taste good and are comfortable to him, rejecting any new or different looking food. Because of a hyper-acute sense of taste the child may quickly detect change within a food that has been carefully supplanted by another in an effort to get him to broaden his diet. His diet may become very limited as a result. This limitation may be carried through into adulthood and can be a very socially restrictive practice. So much of socialising occurs around food and if eating the same foodstuffs as others is a problem then this becomes an additional barrier to spending social time with people. It also has huge implications for maintaining good health and avoiding obesity.

I shared how I tackled this difficulty in the first book *Successful Social Stories™ for Young Children*. Social Stories™ can combine sentences about the past with sentences about the present, and with sentences about the future. This allows the author to help the reader (the audience of the Story) to recall events or achievements in the past to help them tackle a challenge they are facing in the present, and also envisage a time in the future when the challenge has been overcome. This is what neurotypicals do when we too are struggling with something. Using our autobiographical memory, we think 'I have done it before, I am finding it difficult now but I will be able to do it in the future.' I wanted to help my son recall a time when he did try a new food and it quickly became a favourite food.

The Story I wrote recalled that when he was a baby he ate baby porridge then tried a Jaffa Cake and Jaffa Cakes became his favourite food. Trying a new food allowed him to make a very important discovery. He may try a new food and maybe find another favourite food! I reduced all pressure on him to quickly decide if he liked or disliked the new food by compiling a plan that allowed him time to get used to the new sensory experience around the food before tasting it. This meant he spent time getting used to the look of it (on a separate plate), the smell of it and the texture of it before he placed a tiny bit in his mouth. By reducing the stress around the process, acknowledging his discomfort as valid, and giving him more comfortable control around the issue he was able to try new foods, albeit slowly (Timmins, 2016, pp.126–133). Today, Mark will eat a reasonable range of vegetables, carbohydrates and protein.

The following article was written after we talked about the *continued* need for a varied diet into adulthood, after the body has stopped growing. It was important to share information about the health needs of the body and to describe the reasons for a varied diet. This built on what he had studied and understood in his biology lessons at school and still remembered. The detail here may not match the needs of other young adults. An Article should contain the detail the adult requires to explain the information in a way that makes sense for them. The autism spectrum is wide and some adults may need a much more simplified version and others a more highly technical version. The wonderful thing about the technique of writing a Social Story™ or Article is that it is written for the individual and therefore it can exactly match his need.

There are many campaigns about healthy living surrounding us today, on the internet, TV, in the newspapers and magazines, but because they are written by neurotypicals for neurotypicals much of the information is less accessible for the person on the autism spectrum. If, for example, the health promotion depicts foods that are disliked or uncomfortable for a person on the autism spectrum to eat, the information that comes along with that image may not be read and understood, or simply dismissed as inaccurate for him. So there is a need to make this important information relevant and accessible for our young adult population.

As an adult, my son naturally has much more choice over what he has for his lunch and dinner. It is easy for him to slip into the habit of requesting the same meal every night because he never becomes bored with a favourite food and without a reason not to do so, this could become a lifelong unhealthy habit. I wanted to introduce him to the idea of variety and 'healthy portions' of the main food groups. To do this I used the National Health Service's *Eatwell Guide* (National Health Service Choices, 2016) as a starting place and reference. The standard 'healthy portion' plate so often displayed in healthy eating advertising included many foods he disliked so this was not useful for him. I needed to make it meaningful *for him.*

I drew a plate with all the foods he liked in their main food groups (see below). The plate had these three groups of food, each on a defined section, to guide portion size. This visual reminder made it easy for him to recall all the foods he enjoyed, some of which he may have forgotten about. He now chooses whatever he likes from each category and is happy to vary them daily, because they are all comfortable foods he likes to eat. It is an easy choice that is respectful of his different perception. Using this I hope he will maintain a healthy, varied diet into adulthood and beyond. The idea of a personalised portion plate is a helpful one, and one we are trying to follow as a family too – like so many things that are helpful for people on the autism spectrum, it's good practice for everyone!

Keeping the body healthy with a varied diet

The human body is made up of many systems. The many systems usually work together so that the body works well. When all the systems are working well the body is described as being in good health.

Some of the systems are: the digestive system, the respiratory system, the cardiovascular system, the locomotor system, the nervous system, the endocrine system and the urinary system.

Each system is made of cells which do a job within that system. Each cell needs special substances to live and grow and work well. These substances are called nutrients. Each type of cell needs its own kind of nutrients.

All the nutrients needed for a healthy body cannot be found in one food. The body and its cells need varied foods to provide all the nutrients. This is the reason that a varied diet is a healthy choice.

I have drawn all the foods I like to eat on the plate below. The plate is divided into three sections. These sections are the three main groups of foods.

One section is for carbohydrate (bread, pasta, cereals, potatoes). One section is for salad, vegetables and fruit. One section is for all protein foods and dairy foods.

I will try to choose something I like from each section for lunch and dinner in an amount guided by the section line. This may remind me how much of each type of food to eat to keep healthy. Choosing a different food from each section every day is a healthy choice.

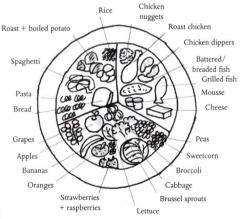

Figure 14: Healthy diet plate

Introduction: What is an annual check-up? / What happens at a health check-up? / Feeling unwell at home – what to do / When to call an ambulance

Recent alarming research has highlighted that people on the autism spectrum have a significantly increased premature mortality from a multitude of medical conditions (Hirvikoski *et al.*, 2016). Further research is ongoing to try to establish the reasons behind this. Meanwhile, we must ensure our young adults have all the relevant information required to improve their chances of living a long and healthy life. Some of this information is around a healthy lifestyle with a varied diet and regular exercise. Other important information concerns the annual health check-up. Each year a check-up appointment is sent by many doctor's surgeries in the UK to young adults with learning disabilities, including those on the autism spectrum.

I have included Articles here to guide my son, and others, on the reason for a health check-up, what happens in a health check-up, what to do when unwell, when to call an ambulance, and how to take medication safely. Attached to the Article on the annual check-up is a checklist of questions to guide the young person through the systems in the body to help locate any problem. This checklist is also attached to the 'What to do when feeling unwell' for the same reason.

Checking one's own body for problems before an annual check-up and at other times is important but there is a careful balance to be struck on how this is addressed. Too much emphasis can generate anxiety and over-zealous checking, leading to an unhealthy obsession with health symptoms and germs. Too little emphasis can lead to changes going unnoticed, which may be signs of a serious but treatable underlying problem if caught early.

Young adults on the autism spectrum are hampered here by their different perception of internal sensation (interoception) (Fiene and Brownlow, 2015). Just as external senses are often heightened, diminished or muddled, and even felt simultaneously all at the same level, so it may be with internal sensations. The autistic brain may perceive a stomach ache as feeling hungry or full when in fact it may be gastroenteritis. The sensation of pain may be ignored or misread, or just difficult to pinpoint, and even broken bones may go unrecognised until someone else notices the disfigurement or lack of function. The kind of sensory dysregulation may be different in each individual. There may be difficulty too in making sense of the internal visceral sensations that contribute to the identification of an emotion that is being felt (Garfinkel *et al.*, 2016). With a lack of contextual information due to context blindness, the ability to identify and label the emotions may be impaired and the person may be consequently unable to communicate how they are feeling to others. This condition is called alexithymia, and it may prevent the patient telling the doctor how he feels emotionally. Accessing medical help can also be hampered by being less inherently mindful of what others know and how they may help, a consequence of a different theory of mind.

It is important to consider the skills required for a young person to access help from a doctor. First, he has to recognise he is ill, then he needs to think that a doctor might help, and consider how urgent that need for help is. He then has to communicate the need for an appointment, get to the appointment and tolerate the surgery noise and queues. In the appointment, he has to understand and answer the doctor's questions and tell the doctor what he feels is wrong. Finally, he has to obtain from a pharmacy a course of medication and safely take it. Even when this is done, he also needs to know what to do if he does not feel better and who to tell, and also what to do if he suddenly feels worse on the medication.

Sometimes a person may feel generally unwell with a cold and need to take a dose of an analgesic and go to bed, having plenty of drinks to keep hydrated. At other times, something more serious is wrong and a doctor's appointment is necessary. My son has had plenty of experience of 'colds' and naturally takes himself off to bed to sleep, so a reference to this within the Article does not need any further explanation. For those who do not know this, another Article will be needed to provide additional explanation.

Very occasionally an ambulance needs to be called as soon as possible. Sometimes we all struggle with the decision on who to call. In all cases, there may be a need for an adult on the autism spectrum to contact his team to request advice. There is a considerable amount of perception, executive function and effective communication involved in all of this, and it is easy to see that without help our adults may fail to access the essential medical care they deserve.

In order for the young adult to access an annual check-up, a caring adult may help him attend and guide him through. It is more important though, and more respectful of the young adult, to show him how to utilise this opportunity himself so that he can keep himself healthy as independently as possible in future.

An annual check-up is important because it gives the medical staff an opportunity to meet the adult when he is well. Over the years, they may get to know him well. This can be extremely helpful if subsequently he becomes unwell, mentally or physically, because the staff have a baseline picture of him. The staff may also be able to notice a difference in his manner or appearance which can flag up a health concern, even if he remains unaware of it. He also becomes familiar with the doctor, the surgery staff and the surgery set-up and so feels less alarmed by it all when there is a need to return when unwell, and perhaps feels more confident to approach the surgery with a health problem. Clarity and predictability help the adult on the autism spectrum manage to navigate the confusing and chaotic neurotypical world.

I devised a checklist of the systems of the body, asking direct literal questions for each system. This list helps focus the attention on how each body system is functioning using simple questions based on the general ideas of whether the system is working, uncomfortable or looking different.

This checklist was also attached to the Articles 'What to do when feeling unwell?' and 'What happens at an annual check-up?' to help pinpoint what area was troubling him in the event of feeling unwell, and also to help him think about any niggling problems before his check-up. The list also made some of the questions that the doctor was likely to ask more predictable and therefore more comfortable to answer.

We talked through what was likely to happen in an annual check-up and jotted down the sequence of events as they happened on the first one. Mark counted how long the discomfort from the blood pressure cuff being tight on his arm lasted (14 seconds) and how long the sting from the cholesterol finger prick test lasted (5 seconds). The second time we attended, everything happened in a very similar sequence. All this information was put into the Article, ready for the following year. I feel confident that this will give him a structure to monitor his health and visit the doctor once a year into the future, without creating too much anxiety.

It is important to note the frequent mention of 'the team' or 'my team' and the advice to inform the team of changes within the young person's life and health. The team around the young adult will be those who care for him and this includes his family members and the professionals involved in his care. Because of the need for vigilance in this group of people regarding healthcare, it is always better to err on the side of caution and this is why I encourage my son and others to tell the team when unwell. This should allow him to access appropriate and timely healthcare, and will also encourage a check to be made on his progress, thereby keeping him safe.

I have also added a short Article on when to call an ambulance. I have been asked several times to write a Social Article for young adults who repeatedly dial 999 for minor ailments. In all these cases the young person concerned had no understanding of what an emergency was. Each young person was experiencing what *felt* like an emergency to him. I think it is important to describe some of the scenarios when an ambulance should be called. That said, if the young adult speaks to someone on their team quickly they can also advise whether an ambulance is required.

What is an annual check-up?

The GP surgery staff want to keep all their patients as healthy as possible. This is the GP surgery's job. To do this, the surgery usually sends an invitation to patients to have a check-up once a year. The purpose of the check-up is to make sure that any health problem is discovered early and treated quickly.

Having a check-up is a chance to check how my body is working and identify any possible glitches that the doctor could help me with. My health checklist (attached) may help me think about each part of my body. I may already have a health worry. Sometimes it is easier to write the worry down than say it. This is okay. I may not have a health worry, and this is okay too.

Having an annual health check-up is like the annual MOT cars have to check they are in good condition and safe to drive on the roads. Attending an annual check-up helps keep my body in a safe and good condition too.

What happens at a health check-up?

At the GP surgery, I usually queue at the desk to speak to the receptionist. When it is my turn I tell the receptionist my name and that I am here for a health check-up with the nurse and doctor. Usually the receptionist will ask me to sit down and wait to be called by the nurse.

It is helpful sometimes to bring something to read or listen to with earphones while I am waiting. Using one earphone usually makes it easier to hear my name when called. The nurse usually calls me first to do a number of checks before I see the doctor.

The nurse usually weighs me and checks my height. This shows whether I am the same weight or gaining weight or losing weight. My blood pressure is also usually measured. This feels like a tight squeeze on my arm for around 14 seconds. Sometimes the nurse also does a finger prick test to measure my blood sugar and blood cholesterol levels. The finger prick test stings for about 5 seconds. When the nurse is finished she usually asks me to sit in the waiting room and wait to be called by the doctor.

When the doctor is ready sometimes he will come and call me, other times a message will flash up on the message board telling me which room to go to, for example, 'Mr T... to Room B to see Dr A...'

The doctor usually asks questions like those on the checklist and maybe some other questions too. This is okay. The doctor wants to know whether I have noticed any problems.

If I am unsure what a question means it is okay to ask the doctor to ask the question in a different way.

When the questions are finished, the doctor usually examines me. Sometimes he examines me on the examination couch. Sometimes he carries out a quicker examination while I am sitting in the chair. The doctor usually decides what he thinks is best.

He may listen to my lungs and heart by using a stethoscope and may feel my tummy with his hand to check it all feels normal. Sometimes the doctor examines my arms and legs and sometimes he may decide that it is not necessary.

Usually the doctor then organises any further checks he thinks are needed. He always checks that any medication I have is prescribed too. Then he says goodbye. The annual check-up lasts about 15–20 minutes altogether. When the check-up is finished, it is time to go home.

Feeling unwell at home – what to do

Most of the time the body is comfortable and all parts work well together. This is described as 'feeling well'. Sometimes the whole body or one part of it is uncomfortable or working less well. This is described as 'feeling unwell' or 'poorly' or 'sick'.

A human body usually repairs itself but occasionally a doctor or nurse may be needed to help the recovery. For this reason, recognising when a part of the body is unwell is important.

Usually when a part of the body is unwell it stops working or feels uncomfortable or looks different. Sometimes it stops working, feels uncomfortable and looks different all at the same time.

The first thing to do when feeling unwell is usually to try to identify the part that needs attention. This is simple if the part is bleeding, or not moving, or looks different, because it is easy to see. If the part is inside the body then using the checklist may help.

Sometimes the body feels unwell all over. Taking the temperature may be helpful. If the temperature is higher than 37.5 degrees it means the body temperature is raised and this may be a sign of an infection. I may use a forehead thermometer to check my temperature and write it down so I can tell my team and my doctor.

Blood may be a sign that there is a problem that needs fixing. Noticing blood in unusual places may help find out the part of the body that is unwell. If I notice blood in my wee, poo, vomit or in what I cough up or blow out of my nose, I may write it down so I can tell my team and my doctor.

Sometimes a person may feel unwell with a cold and after a day or two feels better. Other times it may be necessary to see the doctor or nurse at the surgery. Very very very occasionally a person may be so unwell that an ambulance is called to take him to hospital. My team can help me decide what to do when I feel unwell.

It is important if I feel unwell to tell a member of my team. My team can advise me whether I need to see a doctor.

I am learning about what to do when unwell at home.

BODY SYSTEM	Yes/No/Not sure/ Comment
Respiratory system	
Do I have a runny or blocked nose?	
Do I have a sore throat or ear?	
Can I breathe okay?	
Does it hurt to breathe?	
Do I have a cough?	
Does it hurt to cough?	
What do I cough up?	
Cardiovascular system	
Do I have pain in my chest, arm or jaw?	
Am I breathless?	
Digestive system	
Do I want to eat?	
Have I vomited?	
Can I eat my food comfortably?	
Can I poo comfortably?	
Does my poo look different?	
Do I have a pain in my stomach?	
Musculoskeletal system	
Can I move my arms and legs comfortably?	
Do my arms and legs work well?	
Do any of my arms and legs feel different?	
Does the skin look red anywhere?	
Nervous system	
Do I have a headache?	
Do I feel dizzy?	
Does anywhere feel numb?	
Can I balance okay?	
Skin	
Do I have a rash or spots anywhere?	
Is my skin uncomfortable or itchy?	
Genitals/Urinary system	
Do I have any pain in my private parts?	
Do my private parts work okay?	
Can I pee comfortably?	

Figure 15: Health checklist

When to call an ambulance

Sometimes a person is *extremely* unwell. The person needs treatment urgently. An ambulance has specially trained staff called the crew or paramedics. The ambulance crew know how to give treatment in the home and while on the way to hospital.

An ambulance is for people who are too sick to get to hospital safely or who need treatment very urgently.

To call an ambulance dial ...[1] An operator will answer the call. The operator has been trained to give advice about what to do while waiting for the ambulance to arrive. The operator will ask for the unwell person's name and address. It is helpful to make sure the door is unlocked so that the ambulance crew can get into the house when they arrive.

Knowing when a person is extremely unwell is sometimes tricky. Usually it is time to call an ambulance when a person:

– has become **very ill very quickly**
– has lost consciousness or is difficult to wake
– has had a head injury
– is bleeding a lot
– has fallen and cannot get up
– cannot breathe
– has chest pain
– is having a fit
– is choking
– has been drowned
– has been burnt badly
– is diabetic and losing consciousness or drowsy
– is giving birth
– has been attacked.

When someone is unwell and I am unsure whether they need an ambulance then dialling ...[2] may help. The operator at ...[2] can advise on whether it is time to call an ambulance.

---

1   Insert emergency dialling code
2   Insert medical advisory helpline code.

Introduction: How to book an appointment with my dentist / What to do when a tooth is uncomfortable

The sensory implications of an uncomfortable tooth or a painful tooth may be more different for a person on the autism spectrum with sensory dysregulation than for a neurotypical person. Combined with a difficulty in accurately locating the origin of pain, a toothache may be extremely distressing. Of course, the best option is prevention, and encouragement to access regular check-ups and carry out good regular dental hygiene is very important. But a good dental hygiene routine may also be difficult for someone who has hypersensitive oral sensations, never mind visiting a dental hygienist, and organising check-ups may be difficult for someone with social anxiety. That said, if a person gets into a regular habit these things may become second nature and help avoid unnecessary distress and discomfort.

The social side of booking an appointment by phone and having a check-up are challenging enough for some but online booking is now available for many dental surgeries which is really helpful.

The difficulty experienced in dealing with the social side of the process may be made worse by any discomfort the person feels. As a consequence, it is highly likely that an adult on the autism spectrum with a toothache will need support in accessing urgent dental appointment and care. Two simple Social Articles describing how to access a check-up and what to do if a tooth is uncomfortable follow here, including a reminder to tell the team around the person who can help. As a young adult, my son has regular dental check-ups and books these appointments himself now. Sometimes a script of what to say on the phone helps anyone making a call, and he occasionally benefits from this too. I want him to have a permanent reference guide for future visits so he can remind himself of what to do and say, whether he is accessing an appointment for a check-up or for a toothache.

How to book an appointment with my dentist

The adult set of teeth are the last set of teeth and need to last for many years. For this reason, taking care of them is important. Brushing twice a day with toothpaste and flossing between the teeth once a day usually keeps teeth clean, healthy, comfortable and working well.

Having a check-up once a year helps discover any problems early. This may help avoid discomfort or pain in a tooth.

The dental surgery usually sends an annual check-up reminder. An appointment can be booked online or by phone.

The online link is: …

The phone number is: …

I usually make an appointment by phone. A receptionist usually answers the phone. To make an appointment I usually tell the receptionist my name and that I wish to make an appointment with my dentist Mr … for a check-up or because I have a painful tooth.

One way of saying this is, 'My name is … I am a patient of Mr … I would like to book an appointment with him please.' I may add 'as soon as possible because I have a painful tooth' if I have toothache.

The receptionist usually gives a date and time an appointment is available. It is sensible to write down the date and time of the appointment to remember it.

What to do when a tooth is uncomfortable

The adult set of teeth are the last set of teeth and need to last for many years. For this reason, taking care of them is important. Brushing twice a day with toothpaste and flossing between the teeth once a day usually keeps teeth clean, healthy, comfortable and working well.

Sometimes a tooth may feel uncomfortable. This may happen just when eating or drinking or may happen at any time. Sometimes it is easy to know which tooth is uncomfortable and other times it is tricky.

There may be several reasons for an uncomfortable tooth. There may be food stuck between the teeth. There may be a hole in a tooth. There may be an infection below the tooth in the gum. Sometimes a tooth may just be an extra sensitive tooth.

The first step to take when a tooth is uncomfortable is to clean the teeth carefully using a toothbrush, toothpaste and flosser. Using a mouth wash may help too. Writing down 'uncomfy tooth' or 'sore tooth' on the planner/diary may help remind me when the tooth started to feel uncomfortable.

If the tooth is still uncomfortable after 24 hours and I have already cleaned it properly it is time to make an appointment with the dentist. The dentist has had specialist training in treating uncomfortable teeth and knows how to make them better. He can easily see inside my mouth to discover what the problem is.

Sometimes a tooth may feel more than uncomfortable. It may feel painful. This is usually a toothache. A toothache means I need to see a dentist *as soon as possible*. When I have a toothache a member of my team may help me contact the dental surgery to arrange an *urgent* appointment with the dentist. Sometimes it is comforting to have someone I trust with me when I visit the dentist. A member of my team may help me get to the dentist too.

Taking a painkiller tablet like paracetamol or ibuprofen may help the pain of a toothache. It is important to take the dose written on the box and to follow these directions.

When I book an urgent appointment for a toothache sometimes it may be with my usual dentist and sometimes it may be with another dentist at the practice. This is okay. All of the dentists at the practice know how to help my tooth feel better.

Introduction: Learning about taking medication / What are antibiotics?

Taking medication correctly is important to be safe and healthy. Under the supervision of family members, a young adult can be reminded to take medication daily in the right dose at the right time. However, for future independence he may need to know for himself the reasons behind taking the correct dose at the correct intervals in order to comply safely. Of course, for some adults there may always be the need for complete supervision with medication. These Articles will not replace sensible supervision for any adult on the autism spectrum. For others though, there are steps we can take as carers, parents or professional team members to help the adult understand more about taking medication. By modelling and repetition the process of taking a prescription to a chemist to have it dispensed can be learned. This process has changed over recent years and is different for different areas in the country. It will undoubtedly change again over the next few years as we move forwards with technology, so it will not be described here.

I want my son to know how to follow the instructions on the medicine leaflet and box once he has got it and it is therefore important to share with him the information that others either inherently know or assimilate – information that may be missing for the person on the autism spectrum.

Once established and in the habit of complying with medication, a young adult may of course develop a side effect of the medication and then be confused as to whether he should continue or stop. Following well-meaning instructions literally would mean continuing no matter what. Stopping suddenly for a minor side effect may mean his condition may get worse. Both can cause serious problems.

Information is key here – information on why a particular dose is prescribed, and also what a side effect is and how to ask for help when a side effect is experienced. Asking for help is frequently a difficulty, which results in our adults trying to solve all problems by themselves, not thinking to ask for anyone else's assistance or struggling to find the right words to do so.

In preparation for independence, work can be done practically whenever a course of medication is prescribed for a young adult, by drawing attention to the *dose and timing* and also to how the instructions detail how the medicine should be taken, i.e. with food, or on an empty stomach. The side effects list found within the instructions in every box of medicine is very long and frequently alarming, and trawling through it all may make anyone decide to refuse to take the medication. Modelling to look just at the most common and serious side effects is usually sufficient. Building the understanding that if one feels worse after starting a medication it is important to stop and ask advice is the way to go.

Because of a systematic way of processing the world a young adult on the autism spectrum may sometimes just increase the dosage themselves if they do not feel better quickly. There are health concerns here and the understanding that the dosage should only be changed by the doctor is important to establish and adhere to.

Learning about taking medication

Sometimes a doctor decides that medicine is needed to help a person get better from an illness. He may prescribe a 'course' of medicine. A course of medicine usually means medicine given for a short time, from a few days to a couple of weeks. For some illnesses medicine is given for months or years. The doctor usually decides how long the person needs to have medicine. Medicines may be liquid or solid tablets or capsules.

When taking a course of medicine, the person usually swallows an amount of medicine, called a dose, one or more times a day.

Medicines usually help heal illnesses of the body or mind. Many medicines have side effects too. A side effect is an unhelpful effect of the medicine on the body or mind. A pharmaceutical chemist has carefully worked out the ideal dose of medicine to achieve the best healing with the least side effects.

The dose of medicine may be different for each person. This is one reason why it is always unsafe to take another person's medicine.

The doctor has been trained to prescribe medicine. Some nurses have also been trained to prescribe medicine. This means they usually know all about medicines and the correct doses for each person.

With each medicine, there are usually written instructions about the number of tablets or amount of liquid to be taken, and how often to take the medicine. Sometimes this is written on the outside of the container, sometimes it is on a paper inside the container. This is important information. Taking more than the correct dose of the medicine may make a person more ill. Taking less than the correct dose may not make the person's illness better. When this information is not available a pharmacist or the GP surgery may help.

When a medicine has a side effect which makes the person feel worse then it is sensible to stop taking the medication and ask for advice as soon as possible. The pharmacist or the surgery will advise on whether it is safe to restart the medicine.

What are antibiotics?

Sometimes the body has an infection. An infection happens when microscopic bugs grow in the body. Usually the body can fight infections and get rid of the bugs. Sometimes the body needs help to fight the infection.

Some medicines help the body to get rid of bugs called bacteria. These medicines are called antibiotics. Antibiotics help the body fight a bacterial infection. Antibiotics need to be at the right concentration level in the body to kill the bacteria causing the infection. This is the reason taking antibiotics according to the instructions is very important.

Completing the whole course of tablets is important too. A half-treated infection may allow some bacteria to survive and grow.

These bacteria may have immunity to the antibiotic. This is called antibiotic resistance. Antibiotic resistance makes some infections difficult to treat in the future. For this reason, a person is usually asked to complete the course even after he starts to feel better. Finishing the course of antibiotics ensures all the bacteria are gone.

I will try to follow the instructions on my antibiotics and complete the course. If I feel worse after taking the medicine I may stop taking the medicine and ask advice as soon as possible. My team, the pharmacist, the practice nurse or my doctor will be happy to give advice. I am learning about taking antibiotics safely and responsibly.

CHAPTER 6

Maintaining Mental Health

Introduction: Keeping a positive balance with variety

Autism brings terrific focus to a particular activity of choice and this is one of the many strengths that comes with the autistic profile. However, because of a comparatively reduced comfort in social activities, and a lack of awareness of time, this may result in prolonged periods spent alone.

It is clear that the internet and the digital world hold a host of advantages for young people on the autism spectrum. The removal of the sometimes difficult to read and uncomfortable face-to-face social interaction is a relief, and the substitution of typing comments and replies allows conversation to be slowed down and visible, giving time to think and type the answers. This is really helpful for those who need a few more seconds or minutes to consciously think through a response. People on the autism spectrum are usually skilled at IT and extremely comfortable using it. The internet can be an effective and welcome way of making social contacts, discussing similar interests and being connected to a much wanted and needed peer group. There is also scope for long-term employment within the IT field.

Spending time online can therefore be a very positive and comfortable experience. However, there is concern around internet safety for all young people and ours are more vulnerable here because of their difficulty in reading the intentions of others, even as adults.

Lone time is an effective, restorative practice for those on the autism spectrum and therefore needs to be in place (Attwood, 2008), but when extensive time is spent alone on one sole activity there is no relief or *balance* from any other quarter and this may lead to low mood in some cases. This is the same for neurotypical people and is a concern too; however, neurotypicals are more likely to have a supportive social group of friends who can balance negative comments or experiences with positive ones, giving perspective by providing an alternative insight into the intentions and motivations of others.

I have noted that for many young adults playing a game online or commenting in an online forum may initially be a very positive experience, with success encouraging further engagement. Inevitably though, as more and more time passes, games become more challenging and online discussions more heated. Frustrations emerge and there is more scope for negative experiences to begin to outweigh the positive experiences, particularly in those who struggle to interpret context.

Achieving a balance of more positive experiences than negative ones has been described as important for mental health (Fredrickson, 2013). In young people on the autism spectrum, who tend to recall and dwell on negative experiences more than their neurotypical peers, this becomes even more important. So to keep a balanced healthy mind there is a need perhaps to encourage the young adult to consider a variety of activities of their own choice and increase the likelihood of positive experiences counterbalancing negative experiences.

Being respectful of the choice of activity according to the young person's individual interest is extremely important. Young adults on the autism spectrum have a right, like all people young and old, to pursue their own individual choice of activities in their own spare time. It is a disrespectful mistake to try to coerce a person on the autism spectrum into an activity that a neurotypical deems relaxing or interesting, assuming they will also find it so. Their unique focus also needs to be allowed, not discouraged, because it is a valuable skill. What I am suggesting here is more a matter of encouraging a balance of activities, *all* of which may involve that focus.

Because of difficulties in planning skills a young adult on the spectrum may need help planning free time to include more than one activity. The phenomenal focus on one activity, particularly one of special interest, along with difficulty in reading and using context, may lead to resistance in transitioning from one activity to another. Even moving to another favourite activity may be uncomfortable, so a written down plan from the start involving two or three activities for an afternoon of free time may be more acceptable and pave the way for the transition. This is best decided by the young adult himself before the first activity is begun, with initial support from a team or family member. This structuring of activities to encourage variety requires practice and does not come naturally, but over time it can become a helpful habit or 'second nature'.

Following visual timetables during childhood and adolescence has usually been helpful in coping with transitions, so this 'timetabling' approach is unlikely to be new. Visual timetables help support a weaker central coherence and context blindness. Previously, as a child, the timetable would include activities that were less interesting and were therefore met with some resistance. In this age group, however, the aim is to respectfully guide the adult's skills in organising his *own* timetable of at least two or three different activities that he enjoys and has chosen, so this may be more acceptable. There is great comfort in structure and order, and provided the activities are feasible, it may be surprisingly easy to follow.

It doesn't matter initially what is chosen as long as the young person is moving from one thing to another, giving his brain a break from one train of thought and engaging in another. Even playing three games, two on one console, one on another, will allow him to engage with different groups at different levels, with different levels of success and potential positive outcomes. Over time, the difference between the type of chosen activities can be expanded if he is comfortable with this.

Most of our young adults know exactly what activities make them feel better and can easily list them when asked. However, some may require support from photographs and visuals to remind them of activities they usually choose to do. The most critical thing is that if they need help identifying these we must not just decide what *we* think relaxes them but instead gather information from the people themselves, and also through observation, as to which chosen activities *they* find relaxing.

It is important to note that there is a big difference between being too anxious to leave the bedroom and staying there because you are absorbed in an activity, although one may lead to the other. To encourage a highly anxious person to leave the room involves considerable work on reducing and managing the core feeling of anxiety and alleviating the fear of the social world outside the room. A young person's room may be the only place he feels completely at peace and totally comfortable, a place of sanctuary. However, sometimes being too isolated in a bedroom may lead to a restriction of activities, even those that the young person has previously enjoyed, and this can easily develop into a 'hermit' like existence. Encouraging at least one activity a day to be carried out outside the room or home is ideal to help prevent this happening.

After my son had a particularly difficult experience online, I talked and drew with him about the amount of time he had spent online in one particular activity alone. Because of his intense focus, and perhaps a lack of time perception, he had lost all sense of the extent of time he had spent there. I shared with him information on the need for more positives to balance negative experience in order for people to mentally thrive, and this interested him. He worked out two lists, one of positive things that had made him feel good during his time online and compared it with a second list of negative things that had made him feel bad during the same time period. The negatives easily outweighed the positives on this occasion. I asked him to draw up a list of other activities he enjoyed, which he did very quickly. Of course, many of the activities were screen related, as this is a comfortable medium for him, but nevertheless they were all slightly different in nature.

We then discussed the need for *variety* of activity as healthy input for the mind, highlighting that sometimes a lack of balance happens when a person is involved in only one activity. Developing a sense of balance often chimes with a logical viewpoint and this followed on from the work we had already done on the need for a healthy diet for a healthy body.

I then wrote a Social Article summarising our discussion that described the information he had been missing about this need for balance and how variety brought a better chance for balance to occur. I attached the list of enjoyable activities he had made too, and a copy of the relevant supportive quotations from the research article. Attaching concrete evidence was always helpful in adulthood as it independently corroborated the information I was sharing with him. The resulting Article was information he had been missing, written in a way that was reassuring, positive and accessible for him at this age.

Sometimes I share Articles by email, other times in hard copy. We initially read it together quietly to check that we both feel all points discussed are included. Sometimes he requests we add a point he found helpful. Having shared the Article in this way, when he was faced with free time I gently encouraged him to organise a plan of two or three activities of his own choice with a time interval marked beside each activity. He discovered for himself that this did indeed keep him feeling more balanced and more positive.

The successful timetable he made was then attached to the Article for reference. He kept the Social Article resource in his room and from time to time, when he needed a refresher he reread it. Mark does not always need to use this strategy nowadays but he knows about it and has the Social Article to read for future use. I hope it will always be a useful guide for him.

It may be that you or your young adult will have a different method of avoiding the negative experiences that may come along with extended time alone on one activity. The method chosen needs to be comfortable for the individual. Mitch Christian, an adult with autism, describes a method he uses to avoid getting stuck on one activity in the book *Been There. Done That. Try This! An Aspie's Guide to Life on Earth* (Attwood, Evans and Lesko, 2014):

> Staying involved in activities that I enjoy on a regular basis is a good way to keep tension from growing inside of me. The trick is to limit myself to certain hours of the day for the fun stuff so that I don't get too stuck on it, and to balance that with chores that break me out of the rut caused by focusing too much on one thing. (p.73)

The Social Article I wrote and used follows here. The first four paragraphs are in the third person and the last two in the first person. The font was Times New Roman and the format in two columns like a newspaper article which has a more adult feel. There were no illustrations. These adaptations to the format helped keep it engaging for its adult reader.

Keeping a positive balance with variety

The human body needs a variety of foods to keep it healthy and working well. The human mind also needs a variety of input to keep it healthy and working well. Keeping the mind healthy is important to feel comfortable. Research has shown that more positive thoughts or experiences are needed than negative thoughts or experiences to feel mentally healthy.

When a person has an intense interest in a specific topic or game it is easy to spend a whole day immersed within it. This is usually so enjoyable! Sometimes, though, it may lead to frustrations or comments which can shift the balance from a positive experience to a negative experience.

Many people find that it helps to try at least two or three different activities a day to keep a balance in the input for the mind. The positive comments or outcomes of one activity usually balance a negative comment or outcome from another.

Some people find it helpful to write a short list of activities down as a reminder, like a timetable. Others find using a timer may help too.

Keeping to a varied mental input may be easier to do than it sounds. Most of the time I like playing many different games on a variety of consoles and online, and watching YouTube channels. I regularly enjoy two sports, fencing and archery. I also usually like watching a variety of wildlife documentaries and comedy programmes as well as films such as the *Lord of the Rings* trilogy. Sometimes I like spending time assembling model kits or designing costumes as well as drawing and playing card games with family and friends.

Making a timetable may help me organise my leisure time and an attached example may be a useful guide. I have many and varied interests!

Introduction: Moving from unsettled to settled – what works for me?

People on the autism spectrum may struggle to identify other people's emotions and many also struggle to identify and name their own emotions. When asked how they feel, although clearly unhappy and even distressed, they may find it difficult to put into words. This is a condition called alexithymia (Attwood, 2008). Some are unable to find any words at all; others like Henny Kupferstein describe in the book, *Been There. Done That. Try This! An Aspie's Guide to Life on Earth* (Attwood, Evans and Lesko, 2014) a vocabulary that exactly works for him but may not always be correctly interpreted by others:

> I use words to describe pictures of my feelings as I see them in my head... Although I don't use the expected 'feely' words, I describe the scene of the emotion, and they can derive their own thoughts about which word best fits that scene. 'After I finished that meeting, I felt like I was seeing splatter red spots.' If they say, 'Oh, you mean furious,' I nod my head submissively. Sure, furious. Yeah. Whatever. Even if it doesn't exactly feel like furious to you, let it go. Accept that they have a word for it, and you have a picture for it, and be grateful that worlds met briefly for a moment. (p.181)

We all know the huge relief we feel on offloading how we feel to someone else, even if no solutions are offered – just being truly understood and listened to by another person often brings substantial comfort. There can be no worse feeling than that no one understands what you are experiencing. Being able to communicate that you are distressed and in need of help is also critical if you are going to access any help. Being able to identify, articulate and analyse your feelings is of course the basis of counselling and cognitive behavioural analysis too.

The starting point of discussions around emotions usually begins with emotion recognition.

In writing Social Stories™ around emotion I have found that young people need to discover what calm feels like for them first and how to get there, before they begin to explore more uncomfortable feelings. People on the autism spectrum are continually trying to make themselves comfortable in a sometimes uncomfortable and inhospitable neurotypical world. Most of their chosen activities will be self-regulating strategies, although they may not initially recognise them as such.

Starting emotional work with a positive emotion is always more comfortable than starting with a more negative emotion, which may cause a person to disengage. To establish an awareness of what the feeling 'calm' felt like for my son, I commented on when he looked relaxed and comfortable while doing an activity of his own choice, just simply saying, 'Mark you look comfy and relaxed – you look calm.' I photographed the moment and built a small book of pictures of him in a calm state doing different soothing activities like stroking the dog, listening to music or watching a favourite DVD. This developed into a Social Story™ called, 'What is calm for me?' and then a subsequent one, 'What does calm down mean?' (Timmins, 2016, pp.35–46). This second Story focused on what 'calm down' means, and what soothing strategies he could use to get to a calmer, more comfortable, state. The strategies were all directly related to the activities he sought out himself to calm himself down at home, just adapted so they were portable and could be used out and about.

I have worked continually hard to engage with him in the fields of interest that are his, using vocabulary and scenarios from that familiar, meaningful and comfortable medium to describe new situations or the unexpected actions of others or their intentions. So when trying to express his feelings, he found it hugely useful to use YouTube clips and song lyrics that were meaningful for him, taken from specific interests he had at the time. I became very used to looking at clips on his phone when he wanted to show me how he felt. This strategy is very helpful for describing how a person feels at any particular moment but is not so good when trying to communicate changing feelings or feelings between the extremes. I wanted to help him understand that there were grades of emotions between the extremes and also that he had some control over his feelings and was capable of helping himself feel better by what he chose to do.

I constructed an emotional scale that was specifically meaningful for him. An emotional scale is a scale used to identify the differing emotions felt in between one emotion and its polar opposite (Attwood, 2008). Having tried an emotional 'thermometer' with numbers and colours, which did not connect well with him, we eventually constructed his own 'Sabiggy scale' together. This consisted of a cardboard scale with a photo of the face of a gentle, calm and friendly dog, called Sabi, on the far-left end and a photo of a hissing volatile reactive cat, called Tiggy, on the opposite far-right end. The animals were well known to us all as a family and definitely had these very defined characteristics. These two poles represented feeling calm and in control at the dog (Sabi) end and feeling overwhelmed and out of control at the cat (Tiggy) end. A photo of Mark's face was stuck on a piece of card and trimmed to his facial outline. Instead of asking him 'How are you feeling?', which he struggled to answer, I could now ask him 'Where are you on the Sabiggy scale?' and hand him the photo card of his face. He was able to place his face card on a part of the scale he felt corresponded with how he was currently feeling. Immediately both Mark and myself knew exactly how he felt. It was a huge relief for him to be able to share this with me. On occasion, he could just walk in from school, college or work and place his face anywhere on the scale, or even off the scale, and both of us knew, without any words being found or exchanged, where he was emotionally.

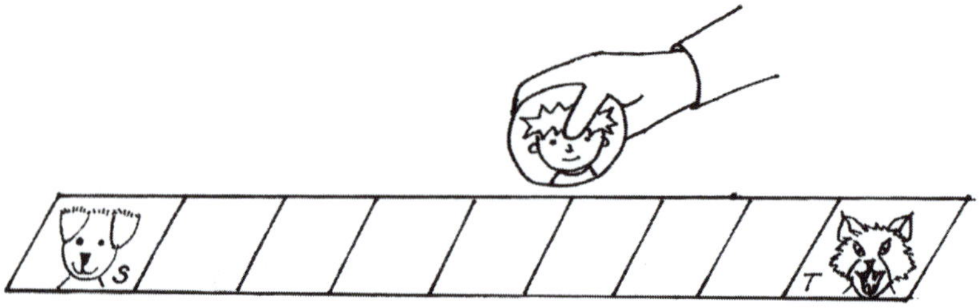

Figure 16: The Sabiggy scale

Knowing where you are on an emotional scale and being able to communicate this with people who care is a huge help. However, being able to improve things for yourself is a step further that is incredibly empowering.

Mark constructed a 'things that make me feel better' list. Then when he placed his face card on the emotional scale to the right of the midline, or even off the scale beyond the cat face, I would gently encourage him to go and choose something *from the list* to do. Having completed his chosen activity, which could be having a bath, or running or watching a much-loved DVD, he would return and place his face card on the scale to show where he was now. Nine times out of ten he would have moved down the scale towards the calm dog end, sometimes by a large amount, sometimes by a small amount.

This simple method concretely demonstrated to him that activities of his own choice helped him move towards calm. He was developing an increased awareness of his own emotions and his own ability to regulate them. In addition, it also allowed me and other members of the family to demonstrate effectively to him and to each other where we currently were on the scale and what we did to move down towards calm.

This scale was used into adulthood. It is still incredibly useful and meaningful for him. I have shared its success with other parents and, in response to their young people's requests, Mark has researched and devised similar scales using, for example, *Pokémon*®

characters at each end depicting emotional states attributed to the characters. One scale had characters from the *Transformer* series, with the characters Optimus Prime at one end and Megatron at the other end. Another had the character Matilda at one end and Miss Trunchbull at the other from the *Matilda* story by Roald Dahl, and another featured *Minecraft* characters. Each scale suited the individual it was made for. Using the special interest made an uncomfortable topic so much easier to approach.

For one young man who loved *Minecraft* I developed a scale using characters from the game. I also copied the 'heart health score' points that feature in the game as a way of measuring the effectiveness of the activities he chose. For each activity on his 'Things that make me feel better' list he awarded a score of heart health points. He could then choose an activity that had, for example, a large heart health score to do when he needed to move a correspondingly large distance on the scale towards the calm and in control end.

Establishing a more complete understanding of a range of emotions between the extremes of emotion requires a professional psychologist or therapist to implement a sequential programme.

For those who are more mathematically able, 'Energy Accounting' may be a helpful method of monitoring and improving mental health. Maja Toudal, an autistic adult from Denmark, first developed the ingenious concept and Tony Attwood has modified its use for his programme to address self-management of depression (Attwood and Garnett, 2016, pp.84–86). This looks at different activities debiting or crediting an internal 'energy account'. When there is a negative balance, more deposits into the energy account are needed, and when an energy depleting activity is imminent, preparation can be made to have sufficient energy in the account first by doing activities that make the person feel comfortable and improve internal energy.

The Social Stories™ initially written for my son about self-regulation during childhood and adolescence needed updating as he became an adult, both with the new strategies he was using and also in a format respectful of his age. Sometimes when feeling unsettled or anxious, listening to a parent, professional or carer's verbal advice may not be helpful. Reading his own Article in his own space and time, describing effective strategies that have worked before, is more accessible for him and respectful too. It aids a self-reflective process that is necessary to build on and develop understanding of self and self-regulation.

Moving from unsettled to settled – what works for me?

In life, every person feels settled some of the time and unsettled some of the time. Every person may also feel settled at one time in a day and unsettled in another part of the day. This is how life is for most people. Usually people have their own way of helping themselves feel more settled. This is often referred to as 'self-regulation'. Some people find this easier to do than others.

Practising techniques to self-regulate is helpful because these techniques are then easier to put into practice when needed.

Feeling unsettled may happen at home from time to time but is much more likely to happen away from home when unexpected things happen.

At home, there are usually several options of activity to help self-regulate but these may be unavailable when away from home. For this reason, having portable strategies is helpful and sensible.

The things that usually work for me currently are:

- the mindfulness technique of four or five slow, deep breaths in through the nose and out through the mouth
- thinking about the episode of *Planet Earth* about the river in the Sundarbans
- listening to the music that goes with this episode
- having a drink of juice.

Sometimes people need more help from their team in order to settle themselves. Telling a member of my team that I am unsettled lets them know that I may need help. It is sometimes tricky to express how I am feeling and if this is the case, using a scale or showing a photo or video may help them understand.

I have a team of people who can help me. They know me and understand me. My team is: Mum, Dad, my brothers and sister-in-law, Dr A and Mrs D.

There are many ways that my team can help me. The first step is to try my own strategies and then alert my team so that they can help me.

Introduction: Anxiety may help sometimes / The human brain has many parts

People on the autism spectrum often describe day-to-day life in a predominantly neurotypical world as continually confusing, uncomfortable and inhospitable, so it is not surprising that they experience chronic anxiety. Therese Jolliffe described how her autism and sensory dysregulation made it difficult for her to work out what reality was: 'Reality to an autistic person is a confusing interacting mass of events, people, places, sounds and sights. There seem to be no clear boundaries, order or meaning to anything' (Jolliffe, Lansdown and Robinson, 1992, p.16).

All brains, both neurotypical and autistic, are wired to notice any change in our environment or in the people around us. This is an instinctual reflex that allows us to respond very quickly in order to avoid or survive a dangerous encounter. This reflex rapidly increases our heart rates and breathing rates so more oxygen is sent to our muscles, getting them prepared for fighting a danger, running away from it or freezing to avoid it. We become hypervigilant, on guard for any signs of increasing danger.

Neurotypical brains are in addition very context sensitive. In a tiny fraction of a second, we are able to read and use the context of a situation in which a change has occurred. We are also able to read the internal context of others. This allows recognition of whether this situation is actually dangerous or not and also recall of previous similar contexts. Not only is the neurotypical brain able to tell the rest of the brain and body to immediately stand down from its hypervigilant state, but it is also able to predict what is going to happen next. This information delivers certainty and reassuring predictability and so anxiety is allayed.

People on the autism spectrum usually have a strong focus on the details of change, partly perhaps because they are inherently less context sensitive. They may be described as 'context blind' (Vermeulen, 2012). As a result, they may be concentrating on a different set of details that attract and interest them rather than the *socially relevant* clues indicated by the context. The autistic brain therefore does not always have the information quickly at hand that reassures that this situation is okay, that there is in fact no danger. It may be much slower to tell the rest of the brain and body to stand down. As a result, the anxious energy levels remain at a high background level.

Some people on the autism spectrum are more able to read context than others, and when things are explicit in familiar situations this difficulty may not arise. That said, nearly all will report a difficulty in understanding the implicit meaning of many situations and interactions.

On top of this generalised anxiety the memory of multiple previous negative experiences adds to the pressure to perform and increases anxiety. We all become more anxious when facing something that we have failed at before, particularly if we remain unclear as to what we did wrong last time. In addition, all of these factors are occurring within a sensory experience that is at best uncomfortable and at worst completely overwhelming. We are often aware of external sensory experiences causing difficulties for autistic people but it is important also to consider the sensations that occur inside the body. The perception of internal sensations in autism, such as the heartbeat, may be magnified so that the experience of an increased heart rate may become really distressing. It is difficult to imagine how anyone could navigate all these difficulties without being chronically anxious.

So how can this anxiety be helped? There are obviously many ways in which sensory dysregulation may be helped by giving due consideration to the possible sensory impact of surroundings with universal design (designed so that they are accessible and comfortable for all people regardless of sex, age, ability or disability), and there are many specific tools or strategies that may be used by the individual to physically reduce sensory overload such as darkened lenses, earphones and pressure vests. There is a great deal that others can do once aware of the problems sensory dysregulation brings. Improving the neurotypical understanding of the different and equally valid perspectives of people on the autism spectrum will bring increased acceptance and consideration in time, and real progress is being made here.

The role of Social Stories™ and Articles here is, as always, to identify and share missing social information with the person. They do so in a format and at a cognitive level that fits the individual exactly, using positive and literal language and illustrations that are meaningful for the individual.

Clarifying the context of situations so that the person can predict what is happening and what is going to happen is really effective in reducing the background anxiety. Neurotypicals also experience anxiety and even panic when they are put in situations they have no experience of and where they are unable to predict what is going to happen. Think back to situations you have been in where you think or say, 'I don't know what to do – I have never been in this situation before!' and remember the anxiety that accompanied it. Social Stories™ and Articles clarify the context by answering key questions – where is this situation, what is this situation, who is here, and who are the key figures, what is going to happen and how, and why? Information may also be shared about what the people in the situation might be thinking, feeling and expecting of others. This information may be unknown or confusing to a person on the autism spectrum. Sharing reassuring social information about what has also *changed* in a situation and what the new situation *now* is can be very reassuring, especially if this information is delivered in a way that is concrete, accessible, positive and respectful, as is required within a Social Story™ Article.

Social Stories™ and Articles can also be written looking back at times when similar problems have occurred, emphasising the successful strategies that were effective, and highlighting the successful outcome. Developing self-reflection in this way builds confidence to tackle a current or future situation, therefore reducing anticipatory anxiety.

A Social Story™ or Article may describe the *purpose* of anxiety, and also describe why anxiety may be heightened for those on the autism spectrum. Understanding this does not necessarily allay anxiety but it does bring meaning to the discomfort, and 'meaningful frustration is easier to bear than meaningless frustration' (Simmons, 2006, p.37). My son, and others, have found having an understanding how their brain interprets the threat of danger surprisingly helpful in coping with their own response to change.

I have found using images from a person's interests helpful in describing different parts of the brain here, and the meerkat is a wonderful example of anxiety personified. I am not alone in this opinion. Jane Evans, a trauma parenting specialist and author, has used the meerkat to personify the survival brain (the reptilian brain) in her book *Little Meerkat's Big Panic*, which although written for young children also has a useful section for older adolescents too (Evans, 2016). Along with using the idea of the 'monkey' brain to describe the thinking brain (the cortex) she also uses the 'elephant' brain to describe the memory of emotions stored in the limbic system. Meerkats also just happen to be one of my son's special interests and have featured in many Stories written about anxiety and change over the years.

The first Article that follows here describes how anxiety is sometimes useful. The second Article uses the concept that a specific area in the brain, which I refer to as the 'survival' brain, behaves just like a meerkat, instantly initiating the fight or flight reflex on seeing a change in the surroundings. Other areas in the 'smart' brain then recognise the context and identify it as safe, telling the survival brain to stand down and relax. To those on the autism spectrum the context is unclear, so the smart brain does not have the information to instruct the survival brain to calm down and as a result the person remains in high vigilance and full of anxiety. This is a simplified description to explain why people on the spectrum may often experience high levels of background anxiety in life.

Included in this Article is a reference to a deep-breathing technique associated with mindfulness. Many research articles have described how mindfulness and deep breathing help move the body towards calm, diminishing symptoms of anxiety and depression. This allows clarity of thought and more conscious planning to occur. It certainly seems to help the symptoms of a pounding heart and fast breathing. For those who are confused by context, and struggle to analyse their own thoughts, a mindfulness approach may bring focus on an identifiable body sensation such as breathing that is something within the person's control. Accepting one's own thoughts and letting them go rather than ruminating over them may break the unhelpful perseverative thought cycle that is often a feature of anxiety in autism. This has been incredibly useful for my son, and he describes it as a 'brain hug' – he enjoys hugs! He practises the technique most days before going out and has an app on his phone that allows him to access a guide to mindful breathing at any time.

Research published in 2013 described how mindfulness-based therapy which had been specifically adapted to take into account the cognitive profile, processing time and language needs of an autistic person was found to be effective in reducing symptoms of anxiety and depression in high-functioning adults with autism (Spek, Van Ham and Nyklicek, 2013). Relevant quotations from this research article were attached to the Social Article.

Many young adults on the spectrum have experienced anxiety as a mind-crushing, overwhelming experience. The very word 'anxiety' itself may fill them with anxiety. To combat this, when talking about how they can begin to reduce their anxiety I often use the words 'settled' and 'unsettled' instead of 'calm' and 'anxious/anxiety'.

It is important to note that these Articles do not intend to, and should not, replace professional help, but they may be useful in helping a young adult understand some elements of his own anxiety and mood and begin to work on helping his own feelings move towards calm. This may help manage anxiety at a stage before any intervention is required or while an appointment is awaited.

Anxiety may help sometimes

When faced with a challenge or something new all people usually feel anxious. This may mean their heart rate goes up, they feel sweaty and shaky and their breathing rate increases. The reason the body does all these things is preparation. The body is preparing for a challenge.

A small amount of anxiety usually helps people feel wide awake and sharpens their thinking. Too much anxiety may cause a panic and a difficulty in thinking.

A small amount of anxiety may feel a little like excitement. This is the reason some people may say they are feeling anxious and are okay with it.

Anxiety is helpful when it improves performance. So sometimes I may feel anxious and it may help my performance. At other times when anxiety gets too much it may be unhelpful and I may need to use my calming strategies to help reduce it.

The human brain has many parts

The human brain has many parts. These parts usually work together to keep the human safe and comfortable.

One part of the brain, the safety brain, notices any change or difference very quickly. Its job is to alert the body quickly to get ready to run away from a potential danger or fight the danger. The safety brain, like a meerkat, is always on guard.

For this reason, when a human sees a change or difference the safety brain is alerted and the heart begins to pump faster and the breathing starts to get quicker. The safety brain is making the body send oxygen to the muscles for running or fighting. This may be an uncomfortable feeling. Many people describe it as feeling very anxious or panicked.

Most changes or differences that the human sees nowadays usually are safe rather than unsafe. It takes a second or two for another part of the brain to recognise that the situation is actually safe. This part of the brain is the smart brain. When the smart brain recognises the situation and is sure there is no danger, it tells the safety brain that all is okay and that there is no need for panic or running or fighting. The heart begins to slow down again and the breathing slows down too. The body returns to normal and feels comfortable again.

People on the neurotypical spectrum usually have a strength in quickly working out whether a situation is safe and predicting what will happen next. Their brain is quick to get the safety brain to calm down.

People on the autism spectrum usually have a strength in focusing on specific details rather than situations. This is part of their many talents and abilities. Their brain therefore may focus on the changing details rather than the situation. This means it may be slower to get the safety brain to calm down. This is one reason why they may spend more time in high levels of anxiety, especially when there is a change.

The good news is that the safety brain will usually calm down if the person takes four or five deep slow breaths (see attached research article). Mindfulness may help too.

I have found that this feels like a brain hug and makes me feel better. I have other strategies that usually help me feel less anxious and calmer. They include:

- recalling a peaceful clip from a wildlife documentary and remembering the music that goes with it
- sipping a juice or water.

The good thing about all these strategies is that I can carry them wherever I go. When something unexpected happens and my safety brain flares up, these strategies usually help calm it long enough for me to think through the situation or ask for clarification from my team.

Using my calming strategies to calm my safety brain usually gives my smart brain time to think.

Introduction: What is a low mood? / Sometimes it's okay just to be okay / What is depression?

Every single person, neurotypical or autistic, in the course of their lifetime will experience episodes of low mood or sadness. Within one single day our mood can change from low mood to okay mood to good mood and back again. When times of low mood go on for a day or two we often describe it as 'feeling down' or 'blue'. The word 'depressed' may also be used colloquially to describe this low mood, which is usually a reaction to a negative experience or life event. This state is, however, usually transient, eventually being alleviated by engaging in distracting activities, talking with friends or loved ones or giving oneself a treat.

The diagnosis of *clinical* depression describes a state of huge emptiness and sadness or very low mood that is not lifted by the usual soothing activities and goes on longer than two weeks. In addition, a person who is clinically depressed will have other symptoms – they may be unable to make decisions, think clearly, go out of the house, eat normally, sleep normally or do anything that normally brings them joy or makes them feel better. A person who feels like this may have thoughts of hurting or killing himself because they find the feeling unbearable and desperately want it to stop.

Most neurotypical people are usually able to recognise their feelings and communicate them to others. Their facial expressions show others how they feel so that colleagues, friends and family members can recognise that they may need help. They can ask others for help and are able to communicate their emotions to professionals trying to help them. Of course, there are some who will struggle to do this but on the whole the capability is inherently there.

Children and adults on the autism spectrum usually have difficulty identifying emotions in other people, and importantly also in themselves. This is a condition called alexithymia, so when in a low mood or depressed they may find it difficult or even impossible to describe how they are feeling to others. They may also be unaware that others may know how to help them and so as a result they may not even think to ask for help or have the words to do so. As a result, they may continue in a state of depression without accessing any help. Along with a difficulty in reading others' facial expressions, people with autism frequently do not show their own emotion using facial expressions. They may therefore feel depressed but not appear depressed to others. Difficulty in reading the context of social situations may result in unexpected responses, so their behaviour may equally not appear depressed to others. Other people may not therefore offer help.

The adult on the autism spectrum may have had many more negative experiences in his lifetime than a neurotypical peer. He may have had numerous social rejections and experienced bullying both in the education system and in the workplace. With impaired or delayed theory of mind he may be less able to distinguish deliberate from accidental harm and therefore may attribute every negative event to having a malicious intention, thus developing a strong sense of paranoia, which can contribute to a depressed state of mind. Impaired or delayed theory of mind may render him less able to imagine how he may feel in the future or even envisage his own future, leading to a belief that he will never feel better. Adults on the autism spectrum are less likely to be in employment, have a long-term partner or close friends, all of which are thought to be protective factors against depression.

For all these reasons, young and old adults on the spectrum may be suffering with poor self-esteem, low mood or depression but neither showing obvious outward signs of it nor requesting help for it, and therefore critically not receiving any.

Depression may have a slow, insidious onset over many weeks and months or it may begin abruptly and become suddenly very severe with the individual expressing immediate suicidal intentions.

This latter type, described as a 'depression attack' by Attwood (Attwood and Garnett, 2016) may be seen more frequently in people on the autism spectrum requiring Level 1 support (previously described as having Asperger syndrome). Although all depression should be taken notice of quickly and action taken to help, the sudden severe depression attack is the one that needs the most rapid response. Because it has come out of the blue, with the person appearing to be quite normal in mood only hours before, the individual may be dismissed as 'attention seeking' by neurotypicals and jollied along or even ignored, which may occasionally result in tragic consequences. I was once asked to write a Story, by school staff, for a young person to 'stop him saying he wants to kill himself' because it was felt to be 'attention-seeking behaviour'. Alarmed by this request I explained that the young man may be trying to communicate his distress and was possibly being ignored because his depression did not 'fit' a neurotypical presentation. I strongly encouraged them to take him very seriously. Fortunately, the staff concerned reviewed the situation and then expedited an urgent assessment for this young man. I subsequently learned that he had successfully accessed urgent treatment shortly afterwards.

Depression and anxiety are the most common psychiatric mood disorders found in high functioning adults and adolescents on the autism spectrum (Hofvander *et al.*, 2009). In research published in 2014, Cassidy *et al.* studied a group of adults who had recently received a diagnosis of Asperger syndrome. Sixty-six per cent of the group had had suicidal thoughts which was more than nine times higher than in the general population and 35 per cent had either planned or attempted suicide during their lifetime (Cassidy *et al.*, 2014). This contributes to the growing body of research indicating that there is an urgent need for increasing awareness, diagnosis and treatment of mental health problems in our young adults. It is clear that helping adults on the autism spectrum with mental health problems requires skilled mental health professionals with specific expertise and experience in understanding the autistic perspective and cognitive processing, and the unique perception of language.

The importance of gathering information from the person via whatever channels they are able to communicate their emotions through is paramount. Use talking, drawing, typing, visual scales or video clips, pictures, photographs or music – whatever makes sense and is meaningful for the individual. It is crucial never to make assumptions from a neurotypical perspective about the intention or motivation behind an autistic response but rather explore it carefully from an autistic perspective. There is a need to be able to ask questions of, and communicate with the person in literally accessible language – language that is not dependent on context for its meaning. It is particularly in this field where the unusual and different thought processes can be easily misunderstood, producing diagnoses and interventions that may be inaccurate and unhelpful. There is inevitably, and unfortunately, a scarcity of mental health professionals with this expertise so there are often long waiting times to access diagnosis and treatment.

The role of Social Articles within the arena of maintaining good mental health remains simple. A Social Article shares missing information with the audience in a meaningful, safe, patient, positive and reassuring manner. As a Social Story™ author, I know that the most important pieces of information about mental health that I need to share with any person on the autism spectrum whether they have, or have not, experienced mental health problems are about understanding the fluidity of mood, how to help oneself move from one mood to another and how to express feelings and ask for help. In addressing these aims I usually try to ensure the young person understands the following:

- People are rarely calm or happy *all* the time, and sometimes it's okay to just be okay.

- All people have times of low mood, normal mood and good mood. Not all low moods result in depression. Moods are usually transient and often all experienced within one day (see 'What is a low mood?').

- There are some simple things that I may do to help myself feel better when I am sad or in a low mood (see 'Moving from unsettled to settled – what works for me').

- It often helps just to let someone know how I feel (using an emotional scale, page 183).

- I may choose words, pictures, video clips, music or a simple scale of emotion to show other people how I am feeling when words are too hard to find.

- When I experience certain changes, I can let my team know and make an appointment with the GP or mental health worker. Knowing what changes to look out for is important for me and my team (see 'What is depression?').

Most of these points can be described in a Social Article, which allows the adult time to read and reflect and refer again to the information. I have included these Articles at the end of this chapter.

Many young people on the autism spectrum may not experience depression in their lifetime. They may still have friends and family who do, however, and having information that depression is an illness like any other, with treatment available, is important. This can stop any misinformation and allay fears that develop around a generally misunderstood illness. A young person who is informed about it, whether autistic or non-autistic, may be able to help another access vital help.

In the Social Article 'What is depression?' I deliberately omit that a low mood needs to be of two weeks' duration or more to be diagnosed as a clinical depression. This is because of the need for extra vigilance in this group of young people. It is important that the team around the young person are alerted at times of low mood whenever this occurs so they can act rapidly in the case of a 'depression attack' where time is of the essence.

Sometimes particular words have negative connotations for young adults. Anxiety and depression may fill a person with anticipatory fear if they have recovered from one episode and fear having another. Choosing alternative vocabulary in a Social Story™ or Article, provided it is understood by the audience it is written for, sometimes allows a sensitive topic to be more comfortable to read about.

Once a clinical depression is experienced, many young adults develop a strong fear of a recurrence and often feel frightened that each low mood they experience will inevitably become a depression. The following Article was written for a young adult who had experienced depression and recovered well but consequently lived in fear of every low mood becoming another depression. It shares important missing information on the normal transient nature of mood.

What is a low mood?

How a person feels inside is sometimes described as his mood. An okay mood usually means he feels settled and okay. A good mood usually means that he feels happy and content. A low mood usually means that he feels unhappy and sad.

A mood is a temporary feeling and one kind of mood usually moves into another kind of mood several times in a day. Movement of mood over time is a daily part of human life.

Many people experience low moods, okay moods and good moods all within a normal day.

I may think of the level of mood as changing continually through the day like a curve on a graph as in the example below. This example shows one day from last week.

Being in an okay or good mood is a comfortable feeling. Being in a low mood is an uncomfortable feeling. When a person is in a low mood they usually want to return to an okay or good mood.

Low moods usually last a short time. Sometimes positive events may lift a low mood back to an okay or good mood. An example may be receiving praise for some work done in the workplace. Choosing soothing activities to do may also lift the low mood back to an okay or good mood. An example may be watching a favourite comedy programme or horse riding.

Movement of mood over time is a daily part of human life.

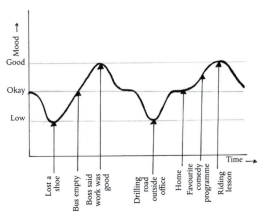

Figure 17: Changing moods throughout one day

Sometimes it's okay to just be okay

Sometimes people feel in a good, happy mood. Sometimes people feel in an okay mood. Sometimes people feel in a low mood. Sometimes people feel settled, sometimes people feel unsettled.

This is okay, this is how life is for many people. It is important to know that while many people strive to be happy all the time people are rarely happy *all* the time. Sometimes it's okay to just be okay.

What is depression?

Most low moods usually get better when a person does his soothing activities. Very occasionally a low mood is not lifted by the usual soothing activities and the person is unable to enjoy his normal interests. He may also have difficulty thinking clearly, making decisions, sleeping or eating too. A person who feels like this usually wants the feeling to stop. This may be an illness called depression.

A depression is a prolonged sadness or low mood that needs the help of a doctor and his team to get better. Depression is a very common illness and most people will experience it in their lifetime. According to the World Health Organization, 350 million people worldwide had depression in 2015. Just like any other illness, it can be treated and made better. There are lots of things the doctor and mental health professionals can do to help.

When I feel in a low mood and it is not soothed by my usual strategies I will try to tell a member of my team or my doctor as soon as possible. This is the first step to feeling better.

Sometimes it is easy to tell another person what I am feeling. Sometimes it is tricky to put it into words. It's okay to choose music, YouTube clips, pictures or photos, drawings or anything else to express how I feel. This helps the person I am telling understand.

When I feel in a low mood and it is not soothed by my usual strategies I will try to tell a member of my team. This is the first step to getting better.

My team is …

I can contact them on …

They will be happy to help me.

CHAPTER 7

Learning about Life Story

Introduction: What is a life story?

I have had a love of reading and writing stories since my early childhood. My love of story remains undiminished today, and I still escape from my daily worries by getting lost in a good book. I believe story to be an inherent part of my nature, and indeed part of *all* human nature. Cavemen told stories and illustrated them on the walls of their caves. Ancient peoples wrote stories on papyrus and parchment. People have always passed on their wisdom and knowledge in stories to the next generation through the spoken word, the written word or through poetry, song and music.

Today, when describing our day to a loved one we do so naturally in story format recounting what happened at the beginning, middle and end. When we explain about life to our children we place our explanations in short stories. When trying to persuade a young person to use caution in a decision we tell stories of good and bad outcomes. When I describe autism to professionals and parents I use real-life stories to to help them understand the points I am making. Politicians tell us the stories of where they have come from to win our vote. We watch films and TV series that are inspirational stories about people's lives. On social media and online blogs people write accounts of the story of their lives and deaths and send it to millions of others to read almost as it happens. Story is, and always has been, an integral part of human experience.

When I first heard Carol Gray talk about social understanding in autism and Social Stories™ I was captivated. I recognised in her description of the different yet equally valid perceptions of the child on the autism spectrum that this was indeed how my son perceived the world. When she described how sharing information could help, provided it was done in a prescribed and respectful way using the Social Story™ approach, I was simply enthralled. Learning how to write Social Stories™ and then practising and using them with my son throughout his life has been effective, enduring and empowering for both of us. It quite simply changed our lives for the better. So when I considered how to inform my son about the major issues of life and death and prepare him as an adult for bereavement I naturally turned to Social Stories™ and Articles.

In our society, death and dying are taboo subjects. Nowadays *being old* is almost beyond discussion. With increasing longevity there is an expectation not only that we will live long lives but that we will maintain youth into old age. There seems to be little regard for the wisdom acquired from a long life that is passed on to the next generation. Much more emphasis is placed on how young an old person looks. Our old people are competing with the middle aged to be youthful in defiance of their age. The topic of aging and dying is avoided in most conversations. When an inevitable bereavement occurs, we are extraordinarily shocked that someone has died, even though we all know we will all definitely die. We cannot bring ourselves even to say the words, and instead use euphemisms to disguise death's reality because it is so painful. We speak in hushed voices that someone has 'lost' a wife or that a brother has 'gone' or 'passed on'. We do this to protect ourselves and others from the hurt that comes with what seems to be brutal and unfamiliar words like 'death', 'dead' or 'died'.

As parents, carers and professionals, we need to think through how the experience of bereavement might be for someone on the autism spectrum. Children and adults on the autism spectrum usually struggle with change. When we consider bereavement as neurotypicals we know that there will be a lot of sudden change, but simultaneously we are also able to predict the course of events and how life will eventually resettle. We will already have been aware that someone has been seriously ill and therefore might die, but this outcome might not occur to the young person on the autism spectrum. It is not usually discussed in an explicit way during an illness and may only be implied by close relatives when cascading news to the family. Implicit clues are often missed by those on the autism spectrum. Following a bereavement, people suddenly use many more words that do not mean what they say. As neurotypicals we read the context, understand the meaning and need no more clarification. Loved ones are visibly distressed, unable to speak and we know and understand why. The normal pattern of life is disrupted with usual enjoyable events suspended and we know why and when they may be reinstated. More people come to the house and visit and we know how long they will stay and what to say to them. Even with all this information to hand, neurotypicals experience great distress when launched into grief.

The young adult on the autism spectrum may not be able to know and understand any of these changes and may not have been aware that any changes were about to take place. Suddenly, out of the blue, life has become unrecognisable for him. And at the heart of all this change is possibly the most devastating change of all. The person who has truly understood, loved and guided that young person from baby to adulthood may no longer be there to explain what is happening or to describe what will happen next and guide him through it. Other equally important people in the young person's life may also be unavailable for him as they struggle with their own grief. It must be completely overwhelming and terrifying. The young adult will feel the same grief but express it in a different way to others, or not be able to understand his feelings and how to express them. Others may misinterpret his emotions.

He may have loads of unanswered questions and be unable to ask even one.

As parents, we cannot predict how our young people will develop, what skills they may learn, what challenges they will be able to overcome, what talents they may have as yet undiscovered, and so we live daily with uncertainty about what adult life may be like for them. The one thing that we do all know with complete certainty is that one day we will die, and we need to prepare them as best we can.

I am frequently asked to help with Stories around bereavement and sadly almost exclusively these Stories are requested when a bereavement has happened or is imminent. Naturally I help as best I am able, but I often think that opportunities have been missed to build understanding for these young people during their early lives, when loved ones are healthy and able to describe these important facts in ways that young people can begin to understand and build on, and share the information that is effortlessly assimilated by their neurotypical peers.

Parents and carers of people on the autism spectrum can begin to explain about the natural cycle of life from an early age, showing how living creatures large and small are born, live and die. The more often this is talked about, the more familiar it becomes. The words become familiar too, and there is less anxiety generated when they are heard. The natural world is a great tutor about life and death. In particular, it explains the purpose of a parent animal in passing on skills for survival and genes for longevity.

For many years, I have talked about wildlife with my son, sitting beside him watching documentaries on various animals together. I am grateful that the natural world is a great interest of his, now more than ever. When watching wildlife documentaries with him I usually comment on or bring his attention to not just the beauty of the natural world but also how the mother animal teaches and prepares the young for independent life when she will inevitably separate from him. Our current favourites are the snow leopard scenes in David Attenborough's *Planet Earth II*. The rarely seen and even more rarely photographed snow leopard is a solitary animal that lives with its mother while fully grown, mastering all the skills it needs to hunt and feed itself before eventually parting from her. These adult cubs stay with their mother for nearly two years and live a total of only 10–12 years in the wild. This strong connection between mother and cub resonates strongly with us both. We watch meerkats too in documentaries like *Meerkat Manor*, where they live in a community together, and we note the community care the meerkats give others in their group, with older siblings caring for younger siblings and watching out for dangers and predators. We talk about how his brothers are similar to the meerkat siblings and I hope we build understanding of the connection of family love. Written into these documentaries are tales of the unexpected death of meerkat pups, adolescent meerkats and old meerkats – sad but incredibly powerful when teaching about life and death.

Over the years my son has witnessed the life and death of a goldfish, a rabbit, a hamster, and three dogs who were not his own (but he loved them nonetheless). There were inevitable changes to note as these family pets moved from being youthful and energetic creatures into middle and old age when their bodies slowed down and they slept more and moved less. Their deaths were difficult to understand at first, but with each one, it became a little less unexpected. Each time a pet died my son experienced loss and sadness, but each time he also recovered from his sadness and was eventually able to talk freely about the pet and remember it fondly without sadness. These pets were not a large part of his life and by their nature (at least the goldfish, rabbit and guinea pig) they did not respond to him with affection and love. The loss of a beloved human is on a different scale.

Mark had never known life without his maternal grandparents and believed they would live forever. Their deaths were huge changes in his life as in their last few years both Granny and Grandad were an everyday part of the family, living next door. One grandparent's death followed the other, only 18 months apart. I was less available for him as I was deep in my own grief. I resolved, however, to prepare him better for the inevitable deaths of other family members and eventually his own parents. I know that no amount of preparation will ever make this easy or comfortable for anyone, autistic or neurotypical, but information must be shared so that our young people are as equally informed as their neurotypical peers.

For my son, the idea of 'life story' is familiar and comfortable. We had talked about the life stories of many famous people on the autism spectrum when we addressed his diagnosis and we read a few life stories too. A story with a beginning, middle and end was a comfortable construct for him. Like many young people on the autism spectrum, he likes to have order, and a feeling of completion was important to him. Describing the end of life as 'finishing the life story' was easy for him to understand. It meant 'job done'. When we closed the book at the end of a story it was finished. He was also very comfortable with the idea of a sequel taking a story into the future, and often recounting the story of the next generation, as in *Star Trek*, *Star Wars*, *The Hobbit* and *Lord of the Rings*, all of which crossed generations and interestingly recorded life journeys on the written page.

Using 'life story' as an analogy for life may not be so helpful for another young adult, and however the reader chooses to address this topic with their young person must uniquely fit him and his understanding. My purpose here is to show that even a topic as challenging as life and death can and should be addressed with sharing information, and that this can be done with a *series* of Stories or Articles over time. Social Stories™ describe life, and death is a part of life.

Because of poor autobiographical memory (Bowler, Gardiner and Grice, 2000) and difficulty recalling socially relevant events, young people on the autism spectrum may need help recalling the sequence of their own life story, and in Stories I have written for my son during his childhood I frequently referred to his growing up and the changes that he had experienced as he grew and his body changed. Tackling old age and bereavement is in a way an extension of that account.

I began by explaining that all of us have a life story, with a beginning, a middle and an end. The beginning of our life story is when we are born and the end comes when we die. And we are all in different parts of our life story at the moment. Each person is unique so we all have different length life stories. Some people are born and die very quickly in infancy, without experiencing any middle life. Some people have a long life story, others have a short life story.

For some who have the comfort of religious faith, the story does not end with the end of life but continues in the presence of their God. For those who do not have a faith there may be comfort in the consideration that at the end of their life stories the wisdom of all living creatures stays with the next generation either through genes or teaching or both. This idea of the transfer of knowledge, wisdom and love may explain the purpose of a life. A well-loved story remains with us for years after we have finished a book, closed the covers and put it back on the shelf. The ideas, wisdom and feelings shared in the story become part of our own knowledge and wisdom and we carry it with us. That's the power of storytelling.

In a similar and simple way, I described that after they have died, parents' and grandparents' love, wisdom and knowledge stay with their children and grandchildren. All that they have taught us remains with us. Their genes remain within their children and grandchildren. They are not forgotten. Despite the loss of their home and possessions at the end of life, all the wisdom and love that they have shared with us during their life stories cannot be taken away. The permanency of this concept is reassuring at a time of huge change. There is a cycle of life, a natural continuation from one generation to the next. This helps us deal with the loss and terrible finality of death, which is so difficult to come to terms with.

As with all concepts I explain to my son, the greatest understanding comes from building on a foundation over time. Cascading training and wisdom is not unfamiliar to him because he has a great interest in Japanese culture and Anime. The Japanese martial arts trainer, or sensei, passes on wisdom and skills to his students in order for the martial art to pass down through the generations. Another translation of sensei is 'one who comes before'. The idea of a trainer training a Pokémon is also one he is very comfortable and familiar with from the *Nintendo* game. By linking these concepts to the visuals of the adult snow leopard mother training her adult cub, I am gradually building understanding using constructs that are interesting and familiar to him.

To describe death and bereavement for other young people on request using Social Stories™ and Articles requires a detailed process of gathering unique information about the young person himself, his interests and usual activities, about the individual who has died, their relationship with the young person and the culture, faith and traditions that they live by. All of these factors will be unique. There can never be a Story or Article that generically describes death and the process of bereavement for every reader; that would be impossible. So here I will share a few examples of how I have *begun* to describe the process of 'life story' to my son. My aim is first to establish a basic understanding of life and death using examples of the losses he has already experienced, and second to develop an understanding of the love, wisdom and training from one generation being gifted to and remaining with the next.

The very first Article in this series begins with a description of life story. It introduces the different length of life story in different species and gives relevant examples of pets my son has known as part of his growing up. This Article introduces the idea of life story for all living creatures using animals that were part of his lived experience.

The second and third Articles shift to the human life story, beginning with 'People have a Life Story too' followed by 'Granny's Life Story'. This is the story of someone he was very close to – his grandmother. It follows a beginning, middle and end format and simply establishes the change in the body's strength and vitality as the person ages. The important information that into old age an older person contributes much to the younger person is also established. It adds that the wisdom, love and genes of the person stay with the next generation after death. At the moment, he does not have a religious faith, but as he grows older he may develop one, and if so the Article will be altered accordingly.

The fourth Article addresses what happens when a life story finishes and a person dies. This Article looks at what happens to the body after death. It refers to his grandparents so is again a lived experience, as it happened for our family. At the time, many other Stories were written in much greater detail about the funeral service, the burial and the wake to prepare him for these which thankfully they did successfully. These Stories were placed with these Articles within the Life Story resource file.

The fifth Article here is about his dog, Rosie. Rosie is his faithful companion and means so much more to him than a pet animal. Rosie is now 12 years old. This story is preparing Mark for when Rosie comes to the end of her life story and dies, which is likely to happen in the next few years. The purpose is to begin to prepare him for this huge change in his life. Avoiding talking about it will not help. Becoming at least familiar if not comfortable with the concept over time may reduce the shock when the inevitable happens. It reminds him of the beginning and middle of Rosie's life and again demonstrates that her body's strength and vitality have visibly changed as she approaches the end of her life story. It highlights that all through her life she has been training her owner and reassures him that her love and wisdom will stay with him when she dies.

We have already discussed with him what may happen after Rosie dies and have decided, with his agreement, to ensure that after a short time of mourning, another dog will take up her place by his side. This will be a great honour for that new puppy! Informing him of what will happen after Rosie has died is extremely important. Knowing what will be the same when big changes occur is hugely reassuring for people on the autism spectrum who may struggle to imagine what the future may be like. Having a plan B for the inevitable end of plan A is of paramount importance. This loss of a beloved companion dog will not equal the loss of a parent but it will give some lived experience of bereavement, and therefore more confidence that after a loved one dies eventually, *in time,* recovery follows. Life goes on, albeit in an altered way.

The final sixth Article is about me, his mum. This describes my life story to date, showing that I am in the middle of my life. The story emphasises that some activities are now difficult for me and I have replaced them with new activities that I enjoy. The Article refers to how I eventually recovered from my own mother's death and how I currently help my son through difficulties and confusions, a training for independent life. The Article will continually be updated as I age, with new ones added, and eventually I will write a final Article, 'What to do when Mum has died'. I have planned to include in this Article what in his life will continue to be the same, as this is very important at a time of massive change, and what he can continue to do, for example the activities he enjoys, that regulate and soothe him. I will include reference to the people on his team so that he will know who can help him with these. He will also be gently guided to take comfort in his family and companion dog and encouraged to discover new things to bring him joy, reflecting back on all the wonderful things he has discovered to do in the past. The Article will remind him that the love and wisdom that I have shared with him are his now and will stay with him and that 50 per cent of all his genes are mine. In this way, I will always be with him.

The following Articles are in a single column format as suits a story format from a book rather than an article from a newspaper or magazine. My son has a good understanding of both the mathematical meaning of 'average' and also the biology of genes so neither of these required any further explanation.

What is a life story?

Every animal on earth has a life story. Every life story has a beginning, middle and end. Every animal begins its life story at the beginning when they are born or hatched and start living. Every animal finishes its life story at the end when they stop living. In between the beginning and the end is the middle of life. Some animals have a short middle of life and some have a long middle of life.

When the life story is finished the body and brain of the animal stop living and cannot restart. This is called being dead. When an animal is dead it cannot breathe or move or see or hear or talk or think or feel pain or pleasure again. The ending part of a life story may be called 'dying'.

The length of the life may sometimes be called the lifetime or the lifespan. Each species of animal has a different average length of life. So some animals have a short life story, others have a longer life story. A few life stories finish unexpectedly in the beginning or middle because of an accident or illness. Most life stories carry on for the average time for that species.

A goldfish usually lives around five to ten years. Squashy, our goldfish had a life story that lasted five years.
A Syrian hamster usually lives around two-and-a-half years. Fuzz, my brother's Syrian hamster had a life story that lasted two-and-a-half years.
A pet rabbit usually lives around eight to twelve years. Pops, our pet rabbit, lived six years.
A Parson-Russell dog usually lives around thirteen to fifteen years. My dog Rosie is now twelve years old.

At the end of a life story in the wild, the love and wisdom of an animal stay with their young in their genes and in the skills the parent animal has taught them. The parent animal is not forgotten because the young use that love, wisdom and their genes to live their own life story.
At the end of an animal's life story as a pet, the love and wisdom of the animal stay with their owner. During the pet's life, the owner usually

learns skills of ownership and receives love and respect from the animal in return. When the animal's life story is finished, the owner remembers the love and wisdom the pet gave him. He may use these skills with his next pet. In this way, the pet is always remembered.

People have a life story too

Every person on earth has a life story. Every person begins their life story when they are born and start living. Every person finishes their life story at the end when they stop living. In between the beginning and the end is the middle of life. Some people have a short middle of life and some have a long middle of life.

When the life story is finished, the body and brain of the person stop living and cannot restart. This is called being dead. When a person is dead they cannot breathe or move or see or hear or talk or think or feel pain or pleasure again. The ending part of a life story may be called 'dying'.

The length of life may sometimes be called the lifetime. People have an *average* lifetime of around 80 years in the UK in 2018. Some people have a longer life story and others have a shorter life story. A few life stories finish unexpectedly in the beginning or middle because of an accident or illness. Most life stories carry on for around the average time.

At the end of a life story the love and wisdom of a parent stays with their young in their genes and in the skills the parent has taught them. The parent is remembered because the young use that love, wisdom and their genes to live their own life story.

Granny's life story

Granny started her life story when she was born in 1926 in Dublin, Ireland. This is a photograph of Granny when she was a baby (photo). Granny had six brothers and sisters. She grew into a child and then a teenager and then a young adult. She was healthy and strong and enjoyed riding a bike and playing tennis! Granny went to school and studied hard and passed her exams.

When Granny was a young adult she went to university to study medicine and met Grandad who was in her year group. This is a picture of Granny and Grandad when they were young adults (photo). When they graduated from university they started work in England. Granny and Grandad got married. This is a photo from their wedding day (photo). Granny and Grandad had two children. One of these children is my mum, Siobhan, the other one is my uncle, John. Granny and Grandad cared for their children until they left home.

Granny spent many years helping my mum with my brothers and me. She loved being our Granny. She always had time to listen to me, time to read me a story, and time to give me a cuddle. Here is a picture of Granny giving me a cuddle (photo). Granny was always pleased to see us. Granny worked in her job as a doctor until she retired when she was 60 years old. She looked after and helped many many children in her work as a doctor.

As Granny got older her body became less agile and strong. She stopped riding a bike and drove a car instead. She stopped playing tennis and did a lot of reading, sewing and knitting instead. This is a picture of Granny knitting a waistcoat (photo). Sometimes in the afternoon she felt tired and needed a nap.

When Granny was an old lady her legs became weak and she was unable to walk far. She used a rollator frame to get around. Grandad and Granny moved next door to us. Every day we brought lunch and supper on a tray to their house next door. Granny told us many stories about her life. She was very good at giving us advice about any decisions we had to make. Granny was always able to help Mum with advice and she always had time to listen to us.

As she got older Granny's lungs were not working well and it became difficult for her to breathe. The doctors gave her medicine and it helped. After a year, the medicine stopped working. Granny's lungs began to stop working. When Granny's lungs stopped working she stopped breathing and she did not start breathing again. The end of Granny's life story came and she died.

Granny's life story ended when she was 78 years old. When Granny died her love and wisdom stayed with all of us who loved her. We all felt very sad because we missed her. Little by little we began to feel less sad. After a while we began to remember the things Granny used to say and they made us smile. We are no longer sad when we think of Granny but smile when we remember the things she used to think, do and say. Granny's love and wisdom stayed with us.

What happens after a life story has finished?

When a life story finishes the brain and the body stop working and cannot be restarted again. This is usually called being dead. When this happens, some people believe that the person's soul or spirit leaves the body behind and goes to be with their God in a place called heaven where living people cannot go. Other people believe that when a person's life story is finished nothing else happens. They believe this is like before the person was born, when they were not alive.

Although the person's life story is finished their body is still precious to the people who loved them. Many people write down what they want to happen to their body after they have died so others will know what to do. Some people ask that when they die they are buried in a special box called a coffin in a special place called a grave. Usually the grave has a headstone with their name on. Others ask to be cremated when they die and their ashes either buried or placed somewhere special to them.

A memorial service often happens before a body is buried or cremated. A memorial service helps everyone recall good memories of the person and celebrate their life story. Sometimes this service is also called a remembrance service, sometimes it is called a funeral service.

Granny and Grandad both wanted their bodies to be buried in a grave with a headstone when they died. Granny and Grandad had a funeral service.

Sometimes on special days like Mother's Day, Father's Day, Christmas Day and on Granny's and Grandad's birthdays Mum visits the grave and puts flowers there. Other people may visit the grave too. There is a bench close by where people may sit and remember them. Some people do not want to visit the grave and this is okay.

When someone's life story is finished the love and wisdom they shared with another person stays with that person. I will always have the love and wisdom Granny and Grandad shared with me.

Rosie's life story so far

Rosie, my Parson-Russell terrier, began her life story when she was born on 7 July 2005. This is a photo of Rosie when she came to live with us as a puppy. She is about ten weeks old in this photo.

Because she was a puppy Rosie played a lot and slept a lot too. All young puppies usually play lots and sleep lots. Little by little as she grew her body became bigger and stronger. She no longer needed naps during the day. Rosie went for walks, chased balls and loved tug of war games. She loved chasing pigeons and squirrels in the garden too.

As an adult dog, Rosie enjoyed agility training, jumping over jumps, running through tunnels and jumping through hoops at speed. Here is a photo of Rosie doing agility training.

She entered a few competitions and won three rosettes. Rosie has grown older and she is now a senior dog. She is much less active. She usually sleeps more during the day. This happens to many animals and humans as they grow older.

Rosie now has cataracts so her eyesight is poor. She still does agility but she goes at a slower speed and over lower jumps. There are still things she can learn and do. She has started to learn new tricks with our dog trainer and last summer Rosie and I achieved a Champion Trick Dog award, winning a huge rosette and a certificate. This is a photo of Rosie and me with the rosette and certificate.

Because of her poor eyesight she sometimes feels uncomfortable when she is left alone or in unfamiliar places, so Rosie usually comes with me on walks in her carry bag and on all our holidays too. Here is a photo of Rosie being carried on a long walk by me on holiday. She usually comes with me when I travel to work every morning too. Rosie usually sleeps in my room now.

Rosie has already had a long and happy life story as my beloved pet. When Rosie's life story ends her wisdom and love will stay with me. She has taught me to be a responsible and good dog owner. She has trained me well! After a while her place at my side may be taken up by another dog. I will try to tell Rosie's life story to the next dog and remember Rosie.

Mum's life story so far

My mum was born in 1959 in Essex. Mum has one older brother. This is a picture of Mum as a baby with her brother and her mum and dad, my granny and grandad (photo).

Mum grew into a little girl and went to school. She learned to play the piano and swim. Swimming and netball were her favourite sports. Mum loved to read books, paint, draw and write stories when she was a little girl. Here are some photos of her as a little girl (photos).

Mum studied hard at school and went to university to study medicine and become a doctor. When she was working in the hospital she met my dad and they got married. Here is a picture of Mum and Dad on their wedding day (photo). Then Mum and Dad had three sons – my brothers and me! This is a picture of Mum, Dad and my brothers and me (photo). Mum stopped working as a doctor and started to work helping children with autism and their families. She looked after my brothers and me at home and a few years later she started to look after Granny and Grandad too.

When Granny came to the end of her life story and died Mum was very sad for a long time. Little by little she began to feel less sad. After a while she began to remember the things Granny used to say and they made her smile. Mum is no longer sad when she thinks of Granny but smiles when she remembers the things they used to do and say. Granny's love and wisdom stayed with Mum. Mum will never forget her mum, my granny.

Mum is now 58 years old. She has finished the beginning of her life story and is now definitely in the middle part of her life story. Some things Mum cannot do any more are headstands, handstands, piggybacks, climbing and rollerblading. Some new skills Mum is learning are sewing, writing books on the computer, and painting watercolours, which she really loves to do. Mum still helps children and adults with autism and their families.

Mum is usually interested in everything I do or think or feel and she loves to write Social Stories™ and Articles to explain anything that's confusing for me. Mum has helped me learn many new things and we usually have fun together. We enjoy making costumes together for the Comic Con each year and watching wildlife documentaries together. All the time Mum is training me for independent adult life, just like the mother snow leopard and her cub.

References

Ali, S. and Frederickson, N. (2006) 'Investigating the evidence base of Social Stories™.' *Educational Psychology in Practice,* 22, 4, 355–377.

Attwood, T. (2008) *The Complete Guide to Asperger Syndrome.* London: Jessica Kingsley Publishers.

Attwood, T. and Garnett, M. (2016) *Exploring Depression and Beating the Blues.* London: Jessica Kingsley Publishers.

Attwood, T., Evans, C.R. and Lesko, A. (eds) (2014) *Been There. Done That. Try This! An Aspie's Guide to Life on Earth.* London: Jessica Kingsley Publishers.

Baron-Cohen, S. (1995) *Mindblindness: An Essay on Autism and Theory of Mind.* Cambridge, MA: MIT Press.

Bowler, D.M., Gardiner, J.M. and Grice, S.J. (2000) 'Episodic memory and remembering in adults with Asperger syndrome.' *Journal of Autism and Developmental Disorders,* 30, 4, 295–304.

Cassidy, S., Bradley, P., Robinson, P., Allison, C., McHugh, M. and Baron-Cohen. S. (2014) 'Suicidal ideation and suicide plans or attempts in adults with Asperger's syndrome attending a specialist diagnostic clinic: a clinical cohort study.' *The Lancet Psychiatry* 1, 2, 142–147.

Department for Work and Pensions (DWP) Waddell, G. and Burton, A.K. (2006) *Is work good for your health and well-being?* Available at: www.gov.uk/government/publications/is-work-good-for-your-health-and-well-being, accessed 7 April 2018.

Evans, J. (2016) *Little Meerkat's Big Panic. A Story About Learning New Ways to Feel Calm.* London: Jessica Kingsley Publishers.

Fiene, L. and Brownlow, C. (2015) 'Investigating interoception and body awareness in adults with and without autism spectrum disorder.' *Autism Research,* 8, 6, 709–716.

Fredrickson, B.L. (2013) 'Updated thinking on positivity ratios.' *American Psychologist.* doi: 10.1037/a0033584.

Frith, U. (2003) *Autism: Explaining the Enigma* (2nd edition). Oxford: Blackwell.

Garfinkel, S.N., Tiley, C., O'Keeffe, S., Harrison, N.A., Seth, A.K. and Critchley, H.D. (2016) 'Discrepancies between dimensions of interoception in autism: implications for emotion and anxiety.' *Biological Psychology*, 114, 117–126.

Goldberg, M., Mostofsky, S., Cutting, L., Mahone, E., Astor, B., Denckla, M. and Landa, R. (2005) 'Subtle executive impairment in children with autism and children with ADHD.' *Journal of Autism and Developmental Disorders*, 35, 279.

Grandin, T. (1996) *Thinking in Pictures and Other Reports from My Life with Autism*. New York, NY: Vintage Books.

Gray, C. (1994) *Comic Strip Conversations*. Arlington, TX: Future Horizons.

Gray, C. (2015) *The New Social Story™ Book* (15th Anniversary edition). Arlington, TX: Future Horizons.

Gray, C. and Garrand, J.D. (1993) 'Social Stories™: improving responses of students with autism with accurate social information.' *Focus on Autism and Other Developmental Disabilities*, 8, 1, 1–10.

Hirvikoski, T., Mittendorfer-Rutz, E., Boman, M., Larsson, H., Lichenstein, P. and Bolte, S. (2016) 'Premature mortality in autism spectrum disorder.' *British Journal of Psychiatry*, 208, 232–238.

Hofvander, B., Delorme, R., Chaste, P., Nyden, A. *et al.* (2009) 'Psychiatric and psychosocial problems in adults with normal-intelligence autism spectrum disorders.' *BMC Psychiatry*, 10, 9–35.

Jolliffe, T., Lansdown, R. and Robinson, T. (1992) 'Autism: a personal account.' *Communication*, 26, 12–19.

National Autism Center (2015) *Findings and Conclusions: National Standards Project, Phase 2*. Available at: www.nationalautismcenter.org/national-standards-project/phase-2/significant-findings, accessed 8 April 2018.

National Health Service Choices (2016). *The Eatwell Guide*. Available at: www.nhs.uk/Livewell/Goodfood/Pages/the-eatwell-guide.aspx, accessed 8 February 2018.

Pate, R.R., Pratt, M., Blair, S.N., Haskell, W.L., Macera, C.A., Bouchard, C. and King, A.C. (1995) 'Physical activity and public health. A recommendation from the Centers for Disease Control and Prevention and the American College of Sports Medicine.' *Journal of the American Medical Association*, 273, 5, 402–407.

Pennington, B.F. and Ozonoff, S. (1996) 'Executive functions and developmental psychopathology.' *Journal of Child Psychology and Psychiatry*, 37, 1, 51–87.

Powers, M.B., Asmundson, G.J.G. and Smits, J.A.J. (2015) 'Exercise for mood and anxiety disorders: the state of the science.' *Cognitive Behavioural Therapy*, 44, 4, 237–239.

Simmons, A. (2006) *The Story Factor: Inspiration, Influence and Persuasion Through the Art of Storytelling* (2nd edition). New York, NY: Hachette.

Spek, A.A., Van Ham, N. and Nyklicek, I. (2013) 'Mindfulness-based therapy in adults with an autism spectrum disorder: a randomized controlled trial.' *Research in Developmental Disabilities*, 34, 1, 246–253.

Timmins, S. (2016) *Successful Social Stories™ for Young Children: Growing Up with Social Stories™*. London: Jessica Kingsley Publishers.

Timmins, S. (2017a) *Successful Social Stories™ for School and College Students with Autism: Growing Up with Social Stories™*. London: Jessica Kingsley Publishers.

Timmins, S. (2017b) *Developing Resilience in Young People with Autism Using Social Stories™*. London: Jessica Kingsley Publishers.

Vermeulen, P. (2012) *Autism as Context Blindness*. Kansas City, KS: AAPC.

World Health Organization (2011) *Global Strategy on Diet, Physical Activity and Health*. Available at: www.who.int/dietphysicalactivity/factsheet_adults/en, accessed 3 February 2018.

Index